GROUNDED IN CHAOS

LEANING INTO ADVERSITY
LEARNING JOY

LISA NEZNESKI

Grounded in Chaos

ISBN-13: 978-1-7347457-0-2

www.529Books.com

Website: www.lisanezneski.com
Facebook: www.Facebook.com/LisaNezneski
Instagram: https://www.instagram.com/lisanezneski/
Twitter: https://twitter.com/LisaNezneski
LinkedIn: https://www.linkedin.com/in/lisa-nezneski-4085b46/

GROUNDED IN CHAOS

Lisa Nezneski

HEALTHY MINDFUL SELF

For Edward Nezneski, who always said,
"It takes a lean horse to win a long race."
I'm in for the long race, Dad.

Note to the Reader

My intention with *Grounded in Chaos* is to increase awareness of how the turmoil brought on by sudden, unexpected change triggers deep emotions. I show how depression feels from the inside out and reveal how I got myself out—so that you, too, can have the world by the ass.

It can be done; I am here.
Be here now.
This is mindfulness at its most reductive essence.

GROUNDED IN CHAOS

Chaos

Chaos theory: within the apparent randomness of chaotic complex systems, there are underlying patterns, constant feedback loops, repetition, self-similarity, fractals, and self-organization.

Chaos

Random.
Random life events.
The randomness of life
As it appears from the inside.
A victim of circumstance,
As it appears from the outside.
Disorder.
Predictable daily patterns
Are thrown out the window.
Nothing is predictable.
All is different and random,
Leading to profound
Confusion.
Disordered thinking.
Depression.
A depressed brain
Trying to make sense of all the disorder.
Rage.
Rage against the disorder
Only leaves you exhausted
And feeling worse.
Vacuum.
What was
Has left a vacuum.

The vacuum is incomprehensible.
You step into the vacuum.
Then you get sucked into the vacuum.
Not by intention.
You get caught up,
And you get defensive.
You try to protect yourself
From all the flying debris
Of the tornado of emotions.
The tornado of depression is destructive.
Self-destructive.
The closer you are to the ground,
The faster the tornado spins
And the more destructive it is.
Floating above the ground
Is not sustainable.
For the first time in your life,
You let vulnerability
Be your friend.
You have no choice but to feel vulnerable
And not push it away.
You welcome the vulnerability
Because it shines a spotlight
On all the unhealed open wounds.
And healing becomes a priority.
Any and all modalities of healing

Become a priority.
You make yourself a priority.
Medication, meditation, Reiki, and prayer.
Grounding.
Place your bare feet on the ground
And feel Mother Earth.
Let Mother Earth welcome
And nurture
In ways your own mother
Was incapable.
Retreat.
You retreat into yourself.
Because the tornado of emotions
Can wound innocent bystanders.
The house can drop on the witch.
Maybe the witch wasn't innocent,
But more external damage
Is not an option.
Dodge the flying debris of
What is left of your life.
Meditation and Mindfulness.
Being aware of what comes up,
Dispassionately examining it.
Take your seat.
Sit and meditate for hours.
First thing in the morning,

Last thing at night.
Prayers all day long.
All the while feeling
The ground beneath
Your feet.
Feeling yourself
Anchored down
Deep to the center of the earth.
Sometimes a waterfall,
Sometimes tree roots,
Most times a giant
Carabiner that clipped
Itself to a rock
At the center of the earth.
A lifeline to catch you
When your feet slip
When you get whipped around
By capricious,
Baseless lawsuits.
When the vicissitudes
Of life surround you,
To encroach on your
Healing space.
Meditation will anchor you.
Prayer will uplift you.
And neither is far from

Daily consciousness
As you mindfully
Observe the past.
As you mindfully
Sit in the now.
Reach to the future.
Be proactive in the now.
And, gradually,
With the hope of each new sunrise,
You begin to
Reassemble order.
The theory of chaos,
The underlying patterns,
The repetition,
The feedback loops
All begin to make sense.
And self-organization
Leads to deeper
Self-understanding.
And, day by day,
Prayer by prayer,
Meditation session by meditation session,
All add up to new perspective.
Perspective leads to
New meaning.
Self-punishment stops.

Forgiveness enters.
Forgiveness of self,
Forgiveness of all others.
Time doesn't heal old wounds,
Forgiveness heals old wounds.
And a new reserve of
Positive emotion
Begins to fill up an empty well.
Drip by drip.
Chaos, the enemy,
Becomes
Chaos, the teacher.
Chaos, the process.
Chaos, the inevitable.
Chaos, the theory.
Chaos, the friend.
The only choice is to befriend chaos.
And, life, once meaningless,
Confusing,
Random,
Insulting,
Becomes
Meaningful,
Intentional,
Wildly circuitous,
Fractal,

Repetitive,
Instructional,
Confusing,
Then clear.
Regression.
Progression.
Moments that are
Wonderfully joyful,
Again.
For the first time.
In the now.

How Did I Even Get Here?

I don't know.
I don't even know
How I let this happen.
Trauma.
Inadvertent trauma.
Unintentional trauma.
Maybe?
I don't know.
In retrospect,
It became the theme.
The underlying theme song.
Sung in four-part harmony.
What do I mean by "it"?
The chaos.
The confusion.
The blindsiding.
Yes, that's it.
Blindsided.
You are driving along,
Working hard,
Head down,
Making it paycheck to paycheck.
Boom.
What do I mean by "boom"?

The administrative assistant calls,
"Jim, the CFO, wants to see you."
And for the next fifteen minutes,
Maybe it was only ten minutes,
It felt like hours,
Time stopped for sure.
My cheeks still get hot just thinking about it.
I suffer the greatest humiliation
Of my professional career.
Eventually, everything,
And I mean every single thing,
That is hidden
Comes to light.
Apparently, I was undergoing
An IRS audit.
Surprise!
Wheeling Hospital received
Notice to garnish my wages.
My wages.
Because I had a job.
Unknown to me,
Was an IRS audit.
That the IRS just got tired
Of unresponsiveness
From the ex-spouse.
And summarily ended it.

No negotiation. No discussion.
Apparently, a lot was
Happening behind my back.
Totally without my knowledge.
I should have gotten a clue then—
The behind my back part.
Too trusting, too understanding,
Too accepting, co-dependent me
Would handle this.
And that is how I lost my house.
Burkes Drive.
I loved that house.
I raised my kids there.
A museum that held
The life of people who no longer lived there,
Overnight became a mausoleum.
And the stress of an already tight
Budget became
Unbearable.
Another challenge.
Another plan.
What do I mean by another challenge, another plan?
Not the first time.
This pattern repeated,
Over and over.
Apparently, this was the lesson

I was to learn.
Can't afford the house.
Sell the house.
That was the plan.
Move to a low-tax area.
Not Butler.
I summarily rejected Butler.
Butler. Really?
Butler would have been better than Rocky Point.
I suggested somewhere warm.
He suggested Wilmington.
And that is how I came to live in
A thirty-two-foot RV for fifteen months,
Behind a warehouse
In an industrial park.
On Castle Hayne Road,
In Wilmington, NC.
And, within two years,
Since that fateful
January day in Jim's office,
I paid back $35K to the IRS.

Hostile Rocky Point

Another challenge.
Another plan.
Find somewhere to live.
Out in the woods sounds nice.
Out in the woods sounds peaceful.
I bought property in Rocky Point, North Carolina.

Not even a wide spot in the road.
It was ten acres of undeveloped land
In the woods, next to Holly Shelter Game Preserve.
Game. Preserve.
Hello? Game. Preserve.

For fifteen months, I pinched every penny to pay back the IRS.
I squeezed those pennies so hard
The boogers came out of Lincoln's nose.

Frozen.
Not the movie.
Try living in an RV in January.
Even the South gets cold in January.
Freeze your ass off sleeping in a sleeping bag.
The time came.

The debt was paid.
The annual bonus arrived.
I start calling around.

Another challenge.
Another plan.
I call the forestry service.
"Can you tell me if the trees are worth anything?"

"Ma'am, it's far season. I can't come and look
Because it's far season."
Oh, FIRE. Fye-yur. Like combustion turned into flame.
My northern ear has to translate. Oy vey.
"When can you come?"
"How about Tuesday, after the fifth Sunday,
When the sun starts rotating backward."
So, while I wait,
Another challenge,
Another plan.
Clear the land.
By this time, it's June.
I should have known
That I should have never moved there.
I arrange to meet a land clearer.
I drive out to the land.
And I wait.

And I wait.
I start to feel sick.
I start to feel really sick.
I start to get sweaty, heart racing sick.
My guts start to swell.

I call the guy.
"Oh, we are so sorry.
Felicia didn't put you on the schedule."
OMG, why is it always so hard with these people???

I drive back twenty minutes to the McDonald's
At the exit on I-40
And I fill the toilet up with bright red blood.

I call the gastroenterologist in Raleigh.
I am diagnosed with Ischemic Bowel.
Of course, I know what that means.
My guts are dying inside
While I am alive.

I should have gotten a clue then.
My body nearly killed me
When I stood on that property.
Before I even moved there.

Another challenge.
Another plan.
But this one took a toll.
I was really, really sick.
But drive on.
There is a challenge to face.
Just now, as I write this,
I wonder what the metaphysical meaning
Of dead bowels means.

"Clear the land."
"Okay," he says, "I got this."
Some boyfriend of the barmaid
At Buddy's will do it.
And that was a complete disaster.
Trees were cut down and piled up
"To be burned."
Stumps weren't removed,
Creating more expense than
If it were done right in the first place.
Because the one quote I got
Was too much money,
Which eventually looked like a bargain.

The day before they plunked down the house
(Just like the *Wizard of Oz*, I swear

It was plunked down),
The guy comes to inspect the land.
And vetoes the whole thing.
"Ma'am, we can't put the house down on all these stumps."
But he can work a deal.
His cousin's brother's uncle's sister's great-nephew
Can come and clear the land.
And I'm stuck.
"So, okay, do it."
The house gets plunked down.
I go to the Midyear Clinical Meeting in Las Vegas.
Because I have to man the booth.
That was the last fun I had for a long time.

I moved into the manufactured home,
And the floor moved when you walked on it.
The floor moved.
In addition to piles of dead wood,
That could harbor vectors of all sorts,
Sand. So much sand.
No yard. Only sand.
This land was apparently part of the ocean at one point.

Sand on everything.
(I am still cleaning sand
That is falling out of my belongings two years later.)

Sand tolerant.
That's how I described it,
How I dealt with it.
I just simply had to tolerate all that stinking sand.
It never went away.
It was always on everything.

And now for the Game Preserve part:
Snakes. Not the friendly little black snake.
Not the friendly little garter snake.
Hostile snakes. Big, hostile snakes.
That owned the land way before I did.
Copperheads, water moccasins were on the land.
I have a deep primal fear of snakes.
I prayed to St. Patrick to
Set up a perimeter around my house
To keep the snakes away, especially when I walked the dog
At night and early in the morning.
It worked.

One neighbor shot and killed
(Yes, with a big frickin' gun) a copperhead.
Came running over to show me the picture.
And, the house 100 yards away killed a water moccasin.
Did I mention that I have a fear of snakes?

Bears.
I went for a walk and saw an interesting big track.
Living in the woods, learning animal tracks
Became a new and necessary skill.
And there it was.
A bear track.
A big, single footprint in the sand.
A big, bear track.
On my land.
Not twenty yards from the front door.
I could have opened the door to a bear.

I could have opened the door to a coyote.
Coyotes howled and yipped every morning and night.
Wild pigs snorted as I walked the dog.
BUGS. If I forgot to spray,
They pounced all over me.
If I forgot to spray my hair,
They bit my scalp.
Mosquitoes as big as dinner plates.
All the mosquito-borne illnesses
Ran through my head:
Malaria, West Nile Virus, Heartworm for the dog,
OMG.

I work from home.
The landline kept going out.
The cell service was spotty.
My workmates would tease me
That I needed to climb the pole
Like in *Green Acres.*
My office was small,
Next to the furnace
That kicked on like the engine of a B-52,
Making it hard to hear the conversations
When the phone line actually did work.
The sun poured into my office window every afternoon.
There was no ceiling fan.

For an entire sweltering summer,
I tolerated a work environment
Without a fan.
He knows a guy.
He'll get a fan.
The fan goes up in the bedroom.
Naturally.
I have to beg for a fan.
He has a cordless one to take to work.
My request goes unanswered.

I worked from home.
I was completely isolated.
I was by myself.
The fire (I mean *far*) department
Would never even know I was back there.
By myself.
Unprotected.
Isolated.
Alone.
And alone in my marriage.

Are you getting the picture?
It was hostile.
Everything about it was hostile.
One day I got in the car
To drive thirty minutes to the grocery store.
When I hit I-40, a scream welled up
From the depths of my soul.
The pain.
I screamed and screamed and screamed
Until I was hoarse.

That was the first week I moved in.
I lasted six months
Until I unraveled.
Rocky Point was not a metaphor.
I lived through the rockiest point of my life.

Silent Desperation

In my silence, I began to despair,
I began to sink,
I began to drown.
And from the bottom of the pool,
I looked up to see a small patch of sky
Shining.
Illuminate the one singular insight,
The one singular dark realization,
That no one needs me,
That no one finds me useful,
And no one cares.

The sun will rise and set
Whether I take a breath or not.

At the bottom of the deep end,
I did not consciously know of the betrayal,
But my bones knew.
My heart knew.
My gut instinct knew.
And my parts all tried to protect me
Like my guts trying to get my attention.
I took a vow.
I did not break that vow.

I loved longer and harder than anything
I have ever done in this life
To find in shock and awe
That I
NO
LONGER
MATTERED.
I had to find how I mattered pretty quickly.

Rejection

The rejection of me
Was complete,
Underscoring my defectiveness.
I am defective.
I am celiac.
I cannot enjoy dinners outside the home.
Underscoring my age,
The bloom is off the rose.
I am post-menopausal.
I am nearly sixty.
I am not in my twenties
But I carry twenty more pounds than I need.
I have dyed gray hair.
I have wrinkles.
I actually like me as that girl:
That chunky, wrinkly, dyed-haired,
Post-menopausal girl,
Until I hate that girl completely.
And, while I worked hard to cope
With an unrelenting illness
That requires vigilance with every bite of food,
With working fulltime from
A hostile environment,
It was all I could do to pull myself together.

And, while I was focused on juggling work,
The hostile environment,
And my health,
I took my eye off the ball.
I had the confidence that thirty-four years of marriage brings
That you handle your shit.
I handle my shit (and your shit).
That the reciprocal dedication to a mutual foundation
Would get us through.
But it was illusory.
It was eroding.
Eroding, but not before my very eyes just yet.
That part came in August.
Meanwhile, I did everything in my power
To make that house work.
I painted every room.
I cleaned all the carpets.
I set up a kitchen in cupboards
That were odd shapes and sizes.
Compromising.
Making it work.
Until it didn't.
Until the rejection was in my face.
I felt a deep resentment growing in him.
Months earlier, I made him get a job

Because the phones got shut off.
The one bill he was supposed to pay.
The phone.
Why was he so eager to pay ONE, and only one, bill?
Whispers,
Whispers to wake up.

Weeds

Isolation became my friend.
Isolation was my companion.
Undeveloped, cleared land
Is quickly reclaimed by tenacious,
Ugly weeds.
Ugly, scraggly, twelve-foot-high weeds.
No exaggeration.
No yard.
Only sand—"solo arena."
Only weeds—"solo malezas."
Si, muy malezas.
Mal, bad.
So, I stayed in the house
Because going outside
Made me feel worse.
Alone.
Isolated.
In the middle of the ten acres,
No one can see weeds.
In the middle of ten acres,
No one can hear you scream.

The Penguins Win the Stanley Cup

I flew to Pittsburgh
For the Penguin's Stanley Cup Championship Parade.
I wasn't missing this parade.
A bright spot in the middle of the summer of 2017.
I needed something to feel better and connected.
Mostly connected.
You can't be more connected
Than being in Pittsburgh for a celebration parade
With one million of your closest Yinzer friends.
I stay at my son's place.
I make him dinner
Because I need to feel maternal.
I had pictures of every single Penguin.
Except Sidney.
I flubbed the pictures of Sidney with the Cup.
Oh well. Maybe a three-peat.
Events were transpiring in North Carolina
Without my conscious knowledge.
What's that saying about the cat being away?
"Go," he says. "Of course, I don't mind."
Of course.
The marriage was on life support.
I just didn't know it yet.
I felt it.

I felt it slipping into my bones.
I felt the downward spiral
That became my depression.

Unraveling

When I moved into the house,
I painted every room.
I wanted a fresh start.
I painted the kitchen blue.
This was the third time I painted a kitchen blue.
Fractal patterns repeating.
There is one window in the kitchen.
I pondered for several months,
The exact window covering that I wanted.
I searched Pinterest for macramé window designs.
I searched. I visualized.
I had an idea.
The perfect shade of blue was in a vest
I knitted years ago.
I searched all through the boxes yet unpacked.
Just as I was about to give up,
The vest showed up.
I loved the ribbon yarn.
I knew it would be the perfect shade of blue,
And, when I saw it, I was proud
That my memory was correct.
I wanted to repurpose
Still closely watching my expenses.
Saturday, July first,

Around 10:00 a.m., he takes off with an
"Okay, see ya later."
I say, "See ya."
No idea where he's going, no idea what he's doing.
Okay, I think, this is weird behavior.
I get pissed.
I start unraveling the knitted vest,
The knits and purls slipping apart,
Leaving a distinct wavy pattern
Like when you unbraid your hair.
I start making the window covering.
Unravel, measure, step up on the footstool, hang it,
Slide the bead on.
Unravel, measure, step up on the footstool, hang it,
Slide the bead on.
Unravel, measure, step up on the footstool, hang it,
Slide the bead on.
For hours, I design the window covering.
All the while, the repetitive action
Puts me in the frame of mind
To feel.
A physically mindful meditative state,
To feel how detached I am.
No one sees.
On ten acres, no one can see
The twelve-foot weeds.

It is a struggle to walk from the car to the house.
I had a thought that week
As I was driving down a tiny backroad—
I thought, I fucking hate living here
With every fiber of my being.
I am shocked by the feeling of hate.
I usually don't let myself go that far.
I usually deal, but not this time.
I experience hate.
I hate everything about this place.
I hate the house.
I hate the drive on shitty, little backroads.
I hate the Podunk post office
That won't deliver packages down my road,
Making me go there during the day
While I work. Closed for lunch. Again.
Why is everything so hard with these people???
I hate the fucking dirt—correction, SAND—road
To my house.
I hate how it floods when it rains.
It rains every day.
It floods every day.
I replace the brakes on my car twice in one year
Because they rusted.
I hate the twenty-eight-minute drive
To the fucking grocery store.

I hate that I have satellite internet that goes out.
I hate that I drop calls all the time,
Making me the butt of all jokes at work.
I hate it here.
I mean, I really hate it here.
And, I hate how he treats me.
I think, I overthink.
I think about the gazebo, still unmade,
In pieces, strewn around the twelve-foot weed- and
stump-filled backyard.
I think about the teak table.
I got a table for free.
I like to eat lunch outside.
The table that I was going to use to paint watercolors,
Sitting in pieces all over the yard.
So, even if I wanted to use it,
It's too destroyed to even set something on.
Because he took it apart.
Ostensibly to fix "this piece of shit."
A favorite invective.
"Piece of shit."
Many times. Many things were "pieces of shit."
I think about the piles of trees,
Still laying around from when the land was cleared.
I think about how afraid I am
After I saw a bear track in the driveway.

I feel the fear of isolation,
The desperate fear of isolation.
I think about the poisonous snakes that the neighbor kills.
"A copperhead prit near big, round as my arm," he said.
He shows me the picture.
I recoil at the sight.
Then he says, "I kilt another,"
And I listened to what he "kilt."
A water moccasin—"About eight feet long."
Did I see it?
He laid it beyond the goat pen.
The goat pen.
My neighbor has goats.
Did I see it?
"No," I say. "You wouldn't catch me looking at a snake,
dead or alive."
St. Patrick is working for me.
How can I be safe?
I am here by myself.
Alone.
All the time.
I think about the chaos all around me.
I think about my sons living their lives.
I think about how I raised them to be independent.
And now they don't need me.
They don't need a mother.

They are grown-ass men—so I'm reminded.
With wives.
With a child.
With careers that make them productive members of society.
I am proud of them.
My boss told me that he hired me
Because I had raised two productive members of society.
I am proud of me.
At least that me.
Because me now is a different me.
They followed in my footsteps.
Although different in their own way.
Following in my medical footsteps.
A nursing executive.
A physician.
I follow this thread of thought as it spirals downward.
Entropy. Or is it enthalpy?
I can't remember.
I can't think straight.
I punish myself for not remembering
A basic scientific fact.
I google it.
Entropy—gradual decline to disorder.
E.N.T.R.O.P.Y.
I slide on downward thoughts about

How I get blindsided.
How only I fix the next thing.
And I fucking hate it here.
All day I think about this shit.
While the knitted vest unravels,
It takes me with it.
It takes me down a dark path.
I hit the point like a coin dropped
Into a funnel-shaped collection container
That spins around in wide circles.
First slowly,
Taking its time.
Then, as the time to make a circle becomes shorter,
As the distance between rotations becomes closer,
The coin speeds up.
Speeding up as it comes closer to the center.
Speeding up as it comes closer to the core.
And, as it takes less time to make a circle,
It travels downward faster,
Until it is spiraling downward so fast
That you can't see it anymore.
It's a blur.
And then it drops out of sight,
Into oblivion.
I hit the point where my thoughts spiral fast.
I decide that the only way out of this fucking mess

Is to step into oblivion.
To end it. Terminally. Myself.
And I can feel my guides and angels surround me.
I feel the hand of God close by.
Hovering closely,
Worried.
Knowing that we have free will.
I recognize all of this from the oblivion.
Deep concern.
Knowing that I am in a dark state,
That I can't even find the words for prayer.
And I feel my guardian angel pray for me—
Help the poor unraveled woman.
The Holy Spirit is nearby.
Praying for me, when I don't have the ability
To assemble a prayer.
I hear the angel say,
"You are not alone.
We are always with you."
1:51 p.m., I receive a text.
I know who it's from,
And I'm not stopping what I'm doing to look at it.
So why update me at 2:00 p.m.
To tell me you won't be around the rest of the day?
I am left alone.
On my own, to do whatever, and wonder.

Around 5:00 p.m., just as I'm ready to walk out the door,
Even in my disordered state,
I put together the thought to get out of the woods.
Drive to the beach. Go to North Topsail.
I pick up phone, keys, and purse, and
He walks in the door.
I am getting ready to walk out.
But I stop. I was in that volcanic mood,
And the pain erupted.
I let him have it.
"You don't need to text me.
You always do whatever the fuck you want.
Don't bother with me.
It is clear I'm not important to you."
I explode.
I erupt, unlike anything I have ever felt before.
I let it fly, "I hate it here.
I hate this place.
I hate how you treat me.
I'm checking out.
I'm giving my grandson the dog
And I'm ending it."
(In my state, the way out of the marriage,
Because "death do us part" is in the vows,
Was to end it.)
I say,

"Nobody needs me.
Wake up!
Our sons are grown men
Who don't need their mother.
We've been here two years,
And no one has come to visit us.
Nobody wants to be around us.
Nobody needs me.
I'm checking out."
Those were my exact words.
"I'm checking out."
This is what depression feels like.
This is what suicidal feels like.
The pain of going on is greater
Than the pain of ending it.
The overwhelming isolation.
The overwhelming aloneness.
The overwhelming feeling of nobody needs me.
The overwhelming feeling of nobody cares.
The world will go on whether I take a breath or not.
At that point in my life, I feel deeply that
There is no reason to go on.
He doesn't care about me.
I tell him this through the cry-talk.
I say, "I can't stand all the shit you put me through."
I say, "I'm just waiting for the other shoe to drop.

What's next?
What is the next shitty thing?
That you will cause that I will have to deal with?
This all started when you humiliated me
By not telling me we were audited by the IRS.
I find out when I get
Called to the CFO's office
Like a kid being called to the principal's office.
The CFO says,
'Were you having an IRS audit? Your wages are garnished.'
WTF?
Year after year, thing after thing,
Shit happens, I deal."
Breathe. Take a breath.
TNTC:
A medical term meaning
Too Numerous To Count.
The things I dealt with were TNTC.
I start back up.
"And over and over
I deal.
This time, for the first time, I'm not dealing.
I don't have any reserves left to deal."
I say, "Nobody needs me."
And he says, "I need you."
"Of course, you do.

IT'S ALWAYS ABOUT YOU."
I say,
"WHAT THE FUCK ABOUT ME?"
Done, nothing left to give.
"I'm leaving. I'm going out to North Topsail."
He says, "I'm going to stay close to you,
So you don't hurt yourself."
"Why?" I say.
"Why?
We aren't working here together.
You coming with me is
Us not working somewhere else."
My depressed brain is not grammatically correct.
I take off.
I drive to the ocean.
I sit on the beach.
And I scream inside.
A primal scream.
I phone my sons.
They each call me back.
But not that day.
Underscoring how alone I am.
And I'm going to die,
Just not that day.

Author's note

Depression, suicidal depression, is a harrowing emotion. And there is an epidemic of people my age ending it. And I get it. But I am here to tell this story and let you know that you are never alone. The National Suicide Prevention Lifeline is 1-800-273-8255. I know how it feels. That's why I'm telling this story. I rebuilt my life. It's a different life, and, yes, that old life did die. But the new life is richer, with more meaning. And, strange as it may sound, I'm grateful for everything I've been through because it brought me here, to today. To tell this story. The story only I can tell, so others may benefit.

In October of 2019, I hung the window covering I made that day. I hung that window covering as a piece of art on an eighteen-foot-high blank wall in my new home in Florida. I tearfully explained what that window covering meant to my new love, and I named that piece "There's Always a Way Out." I see it today as a thing of beauty. Even in my darkest hours, I used pain to create. I look at it multiple times a day and say, "I'm never alone. I'm still here. Now."

Trying to Find Lisa

I spend time trying to find myself.
Saturday was July first,
The day of unraveling.
July Fourth was Tuesday.
I called a therapist's office over the weekend.
I must have sounded pathetic.
They gave me the very first appointment available.
I saw my therapist for the first time on
Wednesday, July fifth, at 11:00 a.m.
We talked about the isolation.
We talked about the raw feelings.
She asked me to write down fifty things that bring me joy.
The only things I could think of were people named Joy.
I wrote their names down.
I couldn't figure out joy as an emotion.
I googled ranges of emotion.
I tried to understand it from a cognitive level.
She asked me to find a picture of myself as a little girl.
She asked me to talk nicer to that little girl.
I found two pictures of myself—
The first-grade picture with the half-smile,
Hiding the bad teeth.
Already at five years old, hiding, disguising shame.
The second picture from some random babysitter—
Me with my right hand clenched

In that familiar gesture I use to release stress.
That started before I was three years old.
I see my little stressed self,
Holding an actual rubber dolly.
A cold, rubber dolly.
No softness in this girl's life,
And me with a familiar squint and no smile.
So, little girl, I am the only one
Who understands
How you feel
From the inside out.
And the therapist
Wants to make a point
That if I feel like
I'm in a dark place,
I can text her.
I file away her card...
Just
In
Case.

Reiki

Over the July Fourth weekend, I called my Reiki girl.
She couldn't see me.
I needed a treatment.
I called the Reiki woman, who I never saw before.
Turns out she was a Reiki Shaman.
She could see me on Saturday, July seventh.
I came to her office.
I sat, she talked as she read my energy.
She said, "You have a serious core."
I agreed, since I was on that quest for joy
And couldn't find it.
I sat, pensive.
She looked shocked and said,
"I feel a primal scream."
I looked at her face
And knew the power of that scream,
And I saw it on her face.
She felt my primal scream.
She said, "Why are you afraid of divorce?"
I said, "What?"
I wasn't even thinking of divorce at that point.
I was thinking, I need to fix myself,
And this was yet another low point in the relationship.
She read me clairvoyantly.

She gave me information
That I did not yet know consciously.
Something is not right in the relationship,
And I'll file that away.
I can't deal with that right now.
Because it's me. I'm having the crisis.
"We are okay." Is that true?
Me immediately rejecting divorce.
What I couldn't articulate at that point
Was that I am not afraid of divorce.
I took a vow.
I'd rather kill myself to end the marriage.
Think about that, Lisa.
Think long and hard about that, Lisa.
What are you really saying?
And I could feel my guides rally around me.
I knew when I said it out loud
That I could make it happen.
I could manifest it.
I already knew I was a powerful manifestor.
I could bring into my life exactly what I needed,
When I needed it.
I was fearfully saying self-destructive things.
And my angels and guides were hovering around me,
Knowing that I had free will.
The Reiki treatment was great at

Calming my turbulent, tornado-like energy.
And I felt sinful.
So far from God.
And I was so depressed.
But Reiki helped.

Work Trip, July 10–12

I have to get my act together.
I have a work trip next week.
I went to Washington, DC for the conference,
Getting my act together,
On a moment to moment basis.
I don't say anything to my workmates.
They don't really notice.
I think they are all in their own ego,
The big national conference,
Where they are seeing and being seen.
Not really noticing me.
Or else I'm faking it pretty well.
I get to the hotel and there is no room for me.
I let the company travel
Make the group hotel reservation.
Somehow, my reservation was missed.
I call company travel and they find me a hotel
Down the street.
I check into an elegant old hotel.
Away from the convention.
I think this is the angels taking care of me.
I'm in a princess room that is quiet, comfortable.
And the energy is calm,
Away from the chaotic energy of the convention.

I fall asleep at 8:00 p.m. and finally sleep.
I get home and tell him I think I pulled it off.
I'm still depressed but no one from my work team
Even noticed me.
Victory or not?
Isolated still, in a crowd of people.
Interesting, I think.

The Escape Pod: The RV

I think I need an escape plan.
Me, still thinking about fixing myself,
Finding myself.
I looked at apartments near North Topsail Beach.
I dismiss it.
I don't want the extra living expense of an apartment.
I need an escape plan.
A literal escape.
I think I can't stand being here,
So why stay?
I can work from anywhere.
I think about this for about two weeks.
Separation and divorce do not enter my mind.
Although, at that point,
The warning from the Reiki woman
Is stuck in my head.
And I watch, observe.
I decide to investigate a small RV.
Not a big, honking Class A
Like the ancient 1994 Class A Mirada
That I lived in for eighteen months.
A little Class C.
A little, girly Class C.
I wake up on Saturday, July fifteenth.

I want to buy my own RV.
I drive to Myrtle Beach.
I have lunch at the Hard Rock Cafe.
I love the energy of Myrtle Beach.
It is palpably different than being out in the middle of ten acres in the woods.
My mood brightens.
On the way down to Myrtle,
I rent a Vacation Rental by Owner for the week of August fifth.
Again, my angels are taking care of me,
Only this time I don't realize it for another two weeks.
I'm going to Myrtle Beach for August fifth
Because my son will be there.
I'll make myself accessible
In case he wants to see me.
I'll work from the beach.
I make it to Camping World
On Dick Pond Road.
I look at two Class C RVs that are about the same price.
Both are used.
One is pristine with 2,000 miles and very simplistic.
One is a couple of years old, well used.
Lots of upgrades but no real table.
If I'm going to work in the RV, I need a table.
I could feel both salesmen,

Leaning toward the bells and whistles
Of the upgraded one.
I chose the simplistic one.
I make a choice for me.
I get approved for financing.
The RV is in my name alone.
The RV is mine.
I drive it,
I drive it well.
I drive it really well.
And I start to feel the elation of freedom.
The name of the RV is *Freedom Elite*.
I notice the freedom part.
The symbolism,
The meaning behind the name.
Weeks later, I think, Yes, I am elite, too.
I have an escape plan.

Visit My Sister

A week later,
It's the last week of July,
I decide to visit my sister.
Watch her kids while I work.
I think I'll spend a week away from Rocky Point.
I'll try to be of service to another,
And maybe connect with my sister.
Her house is chaos.
Her house is a mess.
There is Shit Piled Everywhere.
I retreat to one of the bedrooms.
I worked from her place.
Her kids sat.
Her kids watched TV.
Her kids had a level of childhood inertia
That I had never experienced.
I had two boys that were always doing.
Her kids were sedentary.
Her kids split their time between Mom and Dad.
Just waiting out the week to go back to Dad's.
Not doing, so as to not bring down the wrath of Mom.
Her kids appeared depressed.
I understand depression.
I see my mother in my sister.

I see myself in her children.
Withdrawing.
Alone, guarded, getting through the day.
I have horrendous glutinous reactions
Because her house is a glutinous mess.
Crumbs, wrappers, trash.
An unholy mess.
I start throwing stuff out.
It's a futile situation.
I'm glad to leave.
I leave on Saturday morning.
I drive home in time for a Reiki appointment.
I come home to find no one there.
I smell perfume in the living room.
I smell perfume in the kitchen.
I smell perfume in the bedroom.
I don't smell perfume in my office or sewing room.
Am I "smelling things" or is this real?
I go outside with the dog.
I come back inside and, definitely,
I smell perfume.

More Unraveling

From the time I get back from my sister's,
For the next two weeks,
My life unfolds
In deliberate and inevitable ways.
Months later,
I recognize that
What I held as core beliefs
About what my life was,
About who I was,
Blew up in my face.
Incontrovertible evidence.
Wake up and read the texts.
I go into full-on fight or flight.
Your life has no foundation.
A cataclysmic, destructive earthquake.
Life in the volcanic caldera
Has led to a massive eruption of emotions.
Hot. Destructive.
It's time to protect yourself.
I watch, observe, and begin to wake up
To what this life was.
I am enslaved.
I have less money than living in Pittsburgh.
I am paying all the bills.

I am out in the wilderness,
Like a pioneer,
Scratching an existence out of the land.
I am alone,
And I am left alone.
The week in Myrtle Beach
Was a flurry of activity.
I worked hard to create a
Separation agreement.
If you really mean
That you will do whatever it takes
To heal,
You will need to do
All the really hard things.
To let go of people, places, and things.
That are, at best, not helping, and
At worst,
Malicious.

Saturday, August 12, 2017
My 34th Wedding Anniversary

Waaanniversary.
Only, I'm not crying.
I'm calm.
I'm exhausted.
I met with him the day before to separate.
He signed the separation agreement.
I'm leaving out all the details of being in
Myrtle Beach for a week.
Three trips back to the lawyer, and on
Friday, August eleventh,
I show him incontrovertible evidence.
The text that ended the marriage.
I'm home by myself, and I pack up his stuff.
I throw into the fire,
The sex toys I'd never seen before,
Found in his nightstand.
I pile his stuff in the living room.
After eleven days of a flurry of activity,
I finally rest.
I don't feel much.
Ambivalence about the anniversary.
I haven't eaten a proper meal in eleven days.
I'm still not hungry.

I lost one pound a day for the first eleven days of August.
I'm spent.
I rest.
I plan to get ready for my big project on Sunday.
I am managing a project in Orlando.
Lisa and the Vice Presidents.
Sounds like a band.

Journal Entry: Orlando

The first trip to Orlando,
The week post-separation,
Was for work.
I think:
Stand on your own two feet.
Maybe he can stand on his own now.
Or not.
Not my problem.
I will thrive and not be exposed
To a constant barrage of negativity.
Only softness surrounds me.
In Florida,
The softness of the August sunshine
Nourishes my soul.
I call out.
I send a message out to God.
Please bring to me
Only those who can foster
My happiness and well-being.
Where can I be of service today?

Who Are You?
(Orlando Journal Entry #2)

I crave sunlight.
We end a bit early,
Near Arnold Palmer Hospital.
When you say Arnold Palmer in Florida,
People think hospital.
When you say Arnold Palmer in Pittsburgh,
People think of the gentleman who was a golfing legend.
Arnold Palmer, the original Ex-Pitt-riate.
I sit outside.
I drink his namesake drink, outside his hospital.
Game of Thrones enters my mind:
Maiden.
Mother.
Crone.
Yep, all of those.
My mind goes to
Brienne of Tarth.
Strong woman,
Oath keeper.
I do love redheads.
Brienne, not so much on the redheads.
Uncentered,
Not grounded.

Knocked off my pilings.
I love the Orlando sun.
And in the warmth of the Orlando sun.
I reach down
To the center of the earth.
To feel the grounding of Mother Earth.
Mother Earth.
Was there ever a Maiden Earth?
Will there be a Crone Earth?
Mother Earth.
I feel her welcoming embrace.
I feel my place on the earth,
And I anchor myself to Orlando.
And, after five more trips to Orlando,
I decide to honor that anchor.
I decide to move to Orlando at the earliest opportunity.

Shock and Awe

When I presented the papers, he was shocked.
He thought it would be an intervention.
He drinks too much.
But his ability to not think clearly
Allowed a strategic advantage.
Trust was gone,
Holding intentions close.
Disclosing with the female power
Of the Valkyrie riding into battle.
I aimed my weapons at his heart.
He aimed his affections at other women.
A betrayal of colossal proportions,
Found me floating for weeks,
In a pool of self-righteous indignation.
Alone.
Utterly alone.
Who's shocked and in awe now?

Journal Entry: 8/29/17

Scribbled in my journal,
On the second of six trips to Orlando,
In all caps.
Like I am screaming at myself.
I yell:
I AM MY TOP PRIORITY.
NO ONE ELSE.
JUST ME.
THIS IS NOT SELFISH.
THIS IS NECESSARY.
And long overdue.

ALONE

IS
BETTER
THAN
A
LIFE
OF
WOE,
I entered in my journal.
Sitting outside in the Florida sun,
Trying hard to convince myself
That this process
Is valuable
To my growth.

An Invitation to Joy

I invite more joy to my life.
Doctors' orders.
I took myself to Florida.
I paid for the vacation.
I took the vacation.
Alone, with Oshie.
Oshie, the dear, sweet wonder dog.
Dutifully performing her duties
As Emotional Support Dog.
I went shopping at Disney Springs.
I bought L'Occitane.
As they lovingly applied the hand massage,
I lost my shit in L'Occitane and they comforted me.
This dear, sweet college student from
Georgetown University,
Working a summer job,
Brought the compassion of human touch,
And she let me cry it out.
I went to the movies at the resort.
I went swimming.
I sat outside and read.
I went to Universal Studios.
And for the first time,
In maybe forever,

I took advantage of being on vacation.
I rested.
I relaxed.
I went shopping.
I felt modestly better.
Definitely less depressed.
And I realize
That not being in NC
Has improved my mood.
I double underscore that one in my journal.
Not being in NC feels so much better.
I walked the dog.
And the dog relaxed too.
But in the background, there were actions.
Change the payment source of my payments,
Review the separation agreement.
What's not done, when will it be done?
So even though the intention was to relax,
A flurry of necessary background actions happened.
I filled the time with busyness
And intermittent scheduled breaks,
Where I put myself on the shelf,
And efforted at relaxing.
An oxymoron of immense proportions.

Alive

I think about the word alive.
Single words pop into my head:
Alone.
Alive.
I am alive.

And I start to spell it out.
I start to come up with words
That reflect how I'm feeling.
A way to redirect my depressed
But healing brain
To the truths that are me.

Alone Ass-kicker

Lonely Loving

Insight Intuitive

Veracity Voluptuous

Ex Exceptional

And I think,
If he is an ex,
That makes me an ex, too.
One of my respected colleagues,
Told me in frustration,
"Lisa, don't introduce me as an expert.
An 'ex' is a has-been,
And a spurt is a drip under pressure."
I'm no has-been.
I'm happening.
I'm an ass-kicking, lovingly intuitive leader, who is exceptionally voluptuous.
And I am alive.

I am alive.
What does alive even mean?
The list on the left popped into my head.

And I think, You can do better than that.
And the list on the right popped into my head.
And I wrote it in the pink journal.

Rather than focus on the negative,
I work hard to redirect myself to more positive thoughts.
It's still early.
The kids say, "Too soon?"

I'm on vacation.
And I am self-critical.
And I am self-absorbed.

It's not a space I play in well.
(I sound like my boss.)
I want to think only about me.

What about me?
What about me?
What. About. Me?

At least I can see that I am still lost.
And I can't find me.
But I am ALIVE.

The Pearl Ring

I couldn't stand my naked left hand.
After thirty-four years of wearing rings,
My hand looks weirdly deformed
With no rings to hide the swollen ring finger joint.
Misshapen.
Vacant.
An old lady's hand.
I took action.
I shopped for a pearl ring.
It had to look just right.
I found a sparkly ring
In the shape of a knot,
As in, "not married."
I bought it.
It was inexpensive and started to lose its sparkle.
Symbolic loss of sparkle.
I needed something better.
I went to Universal Studios.
To the pearl place.
The pearl place?
You know, the place where you pick your own pearl.
Out of an oyster sitting in saltwater,
I picked one with an ugly shell.
And out came a nearly perfect

Off-white pearl.
I had it set in a sun-shaped ring, surrounded by diamonds.
Because I am worth more than one diamond.
And the grain of sand,
After years of irritation inside the oyster,
That developed into a pearl,
Is symbolic of the life I lead.
I wear a pearl ring.
In the place a single diamond once occupied.
And it reminds me
That I can turn years of irritation
Into a thing of beauty.

More Therapy

Reiki
Therapy.
Reiki.
I come back from Orlando.
I take off,
Three days in the RV.
My first solo trip in the RV in September.
I get away from Rocky Point.
And I feel peace.
But then I escalate,
I lose my shit.
I'm efforting to write a final report for work.
Everything I write is being rewritten
By "the guy who tells me what to do."
And I feel invalidated.
I hold it together.
Not really.
But I beg for forgiveness from a person
Who I realize was not the problem.
I was. And I learned my lesson.
Walk it off. Read each email twice.
I barely keep it together.
Until Friday, when I go to the therapist.
I'm unraveled. Again.
The therapist says, "I've been expecting this."

She says this is normal.
I say, "It feels awful."
I find my shit.
Somewhere in the middle of that therapy session,
My shit reassembled.
Because, somehow, I handle my shit.
My boss gives me positive feedback,
And it feels good.
Presentation of the big project on Monday.
The team agrees to meet on Sunday.
But I have to show the house.
The invasive, life-interrupting,
Someone wants to see your house.
I cut off the meeting early, so I can vacate the house.
People are coming to look.
I can't stand being there anyway.
And I go back to the ocean.
For about three days,
Out in the RV again.
Where I work, walk, work, walk, work.
Topsail beach.
A preview of North Topsail.
Shit reassembling while I walk on every grain of sand.
Then back home.
Then to my sister's.
Shit disassembling.

What Now?

First the joy,
Then the depression.
Then the joy again,
I am again joyful.
I understand joy for the first time ever.
I pendulate like Foucault's pendulum in the
Pittsburgh Science Center.
Marriage.
First, it's all love, n'at.
It's a financial agreement.
Then it becomes toil.
And then it becomes drudgery.
And, finally, an enslavement
From which you cannot escape.
Until incontrovertible evidence opens the door out.

Give Unconditionally

Why can't I give?
I can't seem to get out of my own mire
And help someone else.
I am the needy one.
But I have no idea what that means.
I am in a tornado of emotions.
And I am barely able to stay attached to the ground.
I can feel myself,
Intermittently disconnecting.
I think it's a good idea to help my sister with her kids.
And that was a disastrous denial of myself.
Again.
That pattern of denying myself,
Because someone I love needs help.
I go, but I am completely incapable.
I'm the one who needs help.
I tell her I can't stay, and my day goes dark.

A Very Dark Day

I wake up sobbing on Tuesday, September twenty-sixth.
And after crying for about an hour,
I get up and go help my sister's kids get ready for school.
I give them each a *Happy Day* note.
I never know what the notes say.
They say *Have a Happy Day*,
And you peel them open
To see the secret message inside.
I made sure to bring them,
To make sure they thought of me,
Wishing them a happy day.
And I think I'll try to make their day a little better.
Meanwhile, my day is slipping rapidly.
I go get gas and coffee and I start to escalate.
I'm driving poorly.
I almost get hit,
Broadside on the driver's side of the car.
I escape, barely.
My brain is not functioning.
Thinking in circles.
I feel so alone,
I start to feel my depression,
Full-on no one needs me,
Suck me downward as negative thoughts

Begin shouting at me from the passenger's seat of the car.
When did negativity get in the car?
At the gas station?
I'm confused.
I hear myself say:
"I don't have a single friend."
And I think it's a good idea to call the ex.
And let him know he won.
He completely destroyed me.
And I'm ready to check out.
Again.
And I check in with a pendulum.
Had I been in Pittsburgh at the Foucault's pendulum,
I would have seen myself pendulating.
But, it was an actual, literal pendulum
That I use when I need intuitive guidance.
Yes or no.
It says "yes" to call him.
And, so, I enter the text: *Can you call me*?
And I sit with the phone,
And I look at it.
I think I'm one of those
Pathetic breakup losers
That can't let go.
And I press send.
And I wait.

He does call back.
And I unravel again.
On the phone.
"What's up?" he says, sort of annoyed,
Like what do ***you*** want, disgusted.
And I tell him I had no one else to call.
I have no friends.
He was my only friend.
With the pathetic cry-talk,
I say, "There is nothing left of me.
I am nothing.
Nobody needs me.
You did this to me.
I did everything for you.
It was always about you.
And you did this to me."
He says, "Where are you?"
I say, "What does that matter?"
And I know that he knows that where I am does matter.
Whoa, my brain is confused. I know that he knows . . .
I'm thinking in circles.
I'm at the place where I was when
He ended the marriage with the
I miss you text to his twenty-six-year-old
"We're just friends."
And I wallow because it's inside my head.

But unspoken.
And I tell him I'm sorry,
I didn't know who to call.
He was my only friend.
And that was the truth.
He says I didn't do anything.
I say he betrayed me in the worst way possible.
Every time I went out of town,
He was chasing tail.
That's how I said it.
He will never apologize.
He maintains that I am the crazy one.
And, guess what?
This is crazy behavior.
But I am so fucking wounded.
I can't help it.
I figure I gotta end the call.
He says, "You need help.
I can't help you."
I say, "I've been in therapy since July.
And it's not helping.
I am nothing.
I'm not getting better.
I'm getting worse."
Because this is going nowhere,
And he doesn't care anyway,

So, I apologize for ruining his day,
And I hang up.
I text my therapist.
I text my sister.
I go back to bed.
I lie there with the lights off.
I sob.
I feel the fabric of my life unravel.
I have this visualization while I lie there, sobbing.
My life was unraveling,
Like when you straighten a piece of fabric.
Row by row, thread by thread is pulled out.
I feel the threads of my life pulled out and
Laying on the floor
In a disorganized heap.
I feel like I am clinging to one thread.
I am a single thread
That is lying on the floor.
I climb inside the thread and sob.
Oshie licks my face,
And then she just lies next to me.
I text my son.
I feel myself unravel.
The fabric of my life is gone.
Unraveled fabric laying in threads on the floor.
I call the suicide hotline,

It's a Pittsburgh hotline,
Because they redirect your calls to your area code,
Really? You could be on the moon.
And the hotline directs you to a local place,
Based on your area code.
The guy from Pittsburgh says he is required
To send my call to someone from South Carolina.
South. Carolina. Where my sister lives.
I say, "Please just talk to me."
I plead. I cry.
"Please, I need to hear someone from the Burg.
I need to talk to a Yinzer."
And then I realize I'm homesick, too.
He puts me on hold. (Really?)
The suicide hotline put me on hold.
Way longer than they should have.
But I figure they are no help.
And I hang up.
I sob some more.
Good thing I brought the little Kleenex packs.
The therapist calls.
She talks to me.
I feel her worry
Through the phone.
I feel her energy,
Excitedly anxious.

Worried.
Like, OMG, this is one of those days
I heard about in school.
Her: One of my patients is in life-threatening distress.
I gotta talk her off the ledge.
Me: I talk to her
For an hour.
Talking in circles, spiraling downward.
I finally reach deep down into myself and say,
"I want to see my grandson grow up.
I want to see him get married.
I want to see his children.
I want to see my great-grandchildren."
And I feel her relax on the phone.
She tells me I'm triggered by being in the chaos
That is my sister and her life.
I agree.
I tell her about this being "the place."
I feel guilty about being away
From Vogler Drive on the day I visited my sister in June.
If I had not been at my sister's,
Would he have had the opportunity?
Would he?
Pointless questions.
And I know it's not my fault.
But yet it triggers the

I'm not good enough.
Not young enough.
Not pretty enough.
Genetically flawed so I can't eat gluten.
Or eggs or chicken or ham or cheese.
And he got fed up with all the structure
I need in my life,
Just to eat without being sick.
And it feeds the *I'm not good enough.*
Why is that my fault?
Why is any of this my fault?
A thirty-four-year marriage.
Each party has a contribution.
A responsibility to contribute.
I am responsible. I contributed.
The 80/20 rule. At least that's how it feels.
And each contributes to the demise.
But this is a primal violation of the vows.
Spaghetti thoughts.
Nonlinear, thoughts that jump from thread to thread.
My son calls me back.
He tells me,
"Get out of that place.
And you need to be in some kind of group therapy,
Because you need to be with people."
I get up. I shower. I try to do something.

I go to the museum.
The Matisse exhibit sucks.
The worst art museum ever
Is in South Carolina.
I couldn't find a single thing to appreciate
While I stood there.
All the Matisse poems are in French. (Really?)
But, outside,
Where I parked my car,
The trees were yarn bombed.
And I think,
This is why I came here.
I was supposed to see the yarn bombing.
And I enjoyed it.
I actually felt a modicum of joy
On the darkest day of my life.
Pendulate much?
I text my sister.
I tell her that I am leaving tomorrow.
I tell her I'll stay until the morning
And help with the kids,
But I have to leave.
So, in her perfectly mercurial way,
She tells me to leave.
Get out now.
She doesn't ask how I am.

She doesn't say anything about the pain I'm in.
Déjà vu.
We have played this drama once before.
Twenty years ago.
And I throw all my stuff in the car,
Buckle the dog into her seat,
And I take off.
Sobbing.

Driving Angels

Trying to pull my shit together.
I say, "Driving angels, you gotta be with me because
I'm not fully here,
And I don't want to have an accident."
I don't know if I actually have driving angels,
But I needed all the spiritual help I could get that day.
And I got it.
About two hours into the drive,
The boss calls.
He wants to know an answer.
I say, "Hey, I gotta go.
I'm going to get pulled over by a cop."
The second ticket in a week.
I got one on the way there.
Driving 60 in a 45 mph zone.
Southern states and driving tickets are like
The sheriff in *Smokey and the Bandit.*
The state policeman pulls out.
I hold my breath,
And he passes me.
I'm speeding, and he caught me.
But he pulls over the car in front of me.
And I thank my driving angels
Because I just got that speeding ticket on Sunday.

I tell Siri to text the boss.
And tell him: *I didn't get the ticket.*
He texts back: *Good Karma.*
He doesn't know about the driving angels,
But yet he knows.
We are all connected.
I just gotta remember that.
I don't know if he believes in Karma.
I stop driving and get him the answer he wanted.
Then I call my son and tell him that I left my sister's.
He tells me that is the best thing I could have done.
I agree.
I listen to him provide thoughtful, reasoned advice.
And all I hear is the love in his voice.
The concern.
The love.
And to know that I can call him during his workday,
And he will answer.
Because I am important to him.
And I feel a modicum of uplift.
I feel.
I love my sons.
My pastor from Pittsburgh calls.
She prays with me.
She reaches out and holds me in the hands of God.
I like her.

She is serious about her faith.
She always says Jee-sus.
She emphasizes both syllables.
And it puts the emphasis on the right thing.
I feel grateful for the prayer.
Because I can't think straight.
About 8:00 p.m., I call the other son.
It's 5:00 p.m. Pacific Time.
He should be done working.
I leave a voice message.
This did not go as planned.
I think I should tell him
I've had another dark day.
He calls back just as I am entering
The driveway to home.
The black hole of my property.
Breaking up, hearing only syllables.
I know I will not have cell signal
If I go any farther.
I've got the phone jammed into my right ear.
And the landline at the house is out again (yes, really).
So, I stop a quarter mile from the house,
In the driveway,
And I try to catch what he is saying.
The breaking up of his voice,
I'm missing words.

But I get one thing loud and clear.
He says, "I'm worried about you, Mom.
The pictures you sent me were disturbing."
A picture of his dad and one of him with his grandad?
Disturbing?
I think.
I listen.
He says, "This is not stable."
And, finally, he hits me square in the solar plexus.
He says, "It is not appropriate for a three-year-old
To be around someone not stable."
Okay.
Wow.
So, it's finally out in the open.
I think.
He has balls.
I'll give him that.
I didn't raise no shrinking violets.
So, the darkest day of my life,
Ends with me being banished from seeing my grandson.
I've been culled from the herd.
No husband.
No sister.
No son.
No grandson.

Thank God at least one son
Is there on the end of the phone.
He has extended a familial lifeline.
A lifeline from the therapist.
A lifeline from the pastor.
On the day I need it most.

Intensive Therapy

I had a work call the next morning after the dark day.
The voice on the phone had such high energy.
Such youthfully exuberant energy,
And the contrast to my mood was palpable.
I made it through the call.
And tried to organize the material that I needed
In follow-up.
And it was like sifting through molasses.
Turgid thinking.
Slow.
The contrast to my feelings was shocking.
I shock myself by how depressed I really am.
And I give myself a break,
I have one more call that day.
I make it through that call.
And I put in for two days of PTO.
The boss approves.
And I get Reiki from the Reiki girl.
She says, "Let's go to the darkness.
You are safe."
Let's go to the darkness.
I let myself go there.
It's the same vision from the very dark day.
It's the edge of a canyon.

She repeats adamantly,
"You are safe.
I am here with you."
She pauses for a breath or two.
"Now, let's step into the darkness."
So, I do.
She says, "What do you see?"
I say, "It's oblivion.
There is absolutely nothing.
It's a complete dissolution of everything."
She says, "How do you look?"
I say, "I am nothing."
I recognize the nothingness.
I flirted with it on the dark day, and on July first.
I am like Voldemort,
Dissolving at the end of *Harry Potter.*
Chunks of me are effervescing off my being.
She says, "Go below the darkness.
Just say what you see."
I see fighting.
I zoom in and I see only redness.
I see demons fighting.
She says, "That's good."
I don't understand why she says that.
She brings me back to the Reiki table.
She says, "You are never alone.

You always have your guides and angels."
Next therapist.
Intensive counseling session
From the psychologist.
I ask her if I'm appropriate for a three-year-old.
She says, "That is utter nonsense.
Have you ever done anything risky around the child?"
I say, "Who, me?
Risk-averse me?
Never."
She says, "This is your son's shit,
Not your shit.
You are an awesome grandma."
And I don't feel it.
But I'm glad that it isn't me.
I only want a relationship.
And the thought that brought me back from oblivion,
On the very dark day was
My grandson.
And wanting to see him grow up.
And now I've been culled from the herd.
I'm floating on an iceberg,
Like an elder eskimo
Who is a burden to the tribe.
Alone to die with dignity.
That thought saddens me.

Profoundly sad,
Depressed to a new level.
The therapist says, "You are never alone.
You can always call me."
Next therapist.
I get Reiki from the Reiki Shaman.
She reads my energy and senses misery.
She senses my weakened state.
She says, "We're going to pull that out of you."
She says, "We're going to download power."
She says the exact three affirmations,
Exactly as I said them as I entered her room:
"I am strong.
I am here.
I am loved."
She downloads power,
And I start to feel so strong.
Pulling me back to myself.
Because ***I am*** strong.
I am kick-ass, take-names, strong.
I've been the strong one in the relationship.
And I'm the one who fell apart.
Because I've pushed the feelings,
Down and down and down,
Deep into my gut,
And now they are exposed.

The Band-Aid was ripped off.
The second I saw "I miss you."
And I am healing.
Healing everything unhealed.
Unsaid, unacknowledged.
And it's all in my face.
The Reiki Shaman says, " You are never alone.
God is always with you.
God loves you."
I stack it all.
I notice how they all repeat the same phrase.
The messages that I need to hear.
In the exact sequence.
Guides, Angels, Professional Help, God.
I'm going to be with my work team next week.
All the therapists say to engage in the energy of my team next week,
When I'm at HQ.
Which was good.
Because the contrast of my mood,
And the palpable excitement of the team,
Even on Friday before the teams meets on Monday,
Was out of synch.
A bit jarring at first.
So, I go with it.

And by Friday night,
I'm feeling infused
With the positive energy transfer
That Reiki Shaman has given me.
And I know that my thoughts,
Are moment to moment choices.
I choose me.
I collapse into bed and sleep.
And I am never alone.

HQ

"Actively listen to the heartbeat of your own 'why'"
Was written on a white board,
On the way to the breakroom,
At the company Headquarters (HQ).
My quest for coffee,
Turned into an affirmation.
Instructions from the universe,
To nurture the why.
I saw myself.
No, I mean I really saw a picture of myself
As I walked down the hall.
I stood mute and smiling in an office
On the way to the breakroom.
My picture from the Wharton School,
Hung in someone's office,
On the way to the breakroom.
And there I was.
Proof that I exist.
In the front row.
Wearing a red sweater.
Smiling.
Smiling a radiant smile.
Because I was a Wharton School graduate.
I hobbed and nobbed with the elite of my company.

My trajectory was upward.
My star was rising.
And I did a good job.
I was proud of myself.
I see myself,
On the day the poem Luminous was written.
Prior to the 30-pound weight loss.
Smiling.
That girl liked herself.
Until she didn't.
There she is.
She can stand in the front row.
Claim herself.
Claim the power of the red sweater.
And go on.
It's time to get over it.
Louise Hay said, "Let that nonsense go".
And it's time.
I'm at HQ.
I belong.
My star is ascending.
And Mike Lange, the Penguins Announcer,
Pops into my head:
"Buckle up, Baby!" It's going to be a bumpy ride.

The CEO

I have the intermittent fantasy,
That someone from work will find me attractive.
Not the guys on my team.
Not that at all.
A powerful executive,
Who sees my value.
And doesn't exploit me.
I think about choices,
That I will make in the next relationship.
I know it's way too early.
I go to lunch.
And as I choose an Honest Tea.
The play on Honesty hits me.
Because he's lied to my face again,
This past weekend before I got on the plane for HQ.
A man steps up next to me
And starts talking about the extensive beverage choices.
I look over and recognize him.
He's the CEO.
And the CEO reaches up and chooses Fiji water.
I smile and say I like Honest Tea.
And tells me how much he likes the Honest Tea green tea.
He says something about another beverage,
And I say that I was a bit disappointed

Because it has artificial sweetener.
He makes a remark about the calorie count on the bottle.
And I feel a bit flirtatious.
With the CEO.
And he was just being nice,
It's his job to chat up the employees.
But being noticed.
Talked to.
Conversed with.
A mindful, I see you moment.
About Honest Tea.
Honesty.
Didn't escape me.
It was a manifestation of the fantasy,
In a way that was safe
And what I needed at that moment.
And it was thrilling.

Weaving

I'm lying on the Reiki table.
As she does her thing,
I get the message
"Weave a new fabric of your life."
And my mind goes to warp and weft.
Under and over.
Under and over.
High points.
Low points.
High points.
Low points.
Like my mood.
Pendulation.
Mountains.
Sea level.
Mountains.
Sea level.
And my eyes pop open.
I tell her about being a thread,
Lying on the floor as a metaphorical single thread.
That I climbed into the thread,
That I told myself I would be the best thread I could be.
That I was just told to "weave a new fabric."
And how I mentally began weaving.

And how it went to highs, and lows.
And to mountains and sea level.
She says you will do well in the mountains.
And I think,
Where should I go next?
Colorado.
Florida.
Colorado.
Florida.
Warp, Weft.
And I think that I am not yet ready to go back to snow.
I think I need to sort through the stuff in storage and
Let it go.
And what is the most practical way to do this.
I don't want to move the stuff I don't want.
Yet again move that stuff.
More mindfully this time.
And she says energetically,
"You are drawn to the mountains."
And I know she's right.
So, as I weave a new fabric.
I need to let the old stash of fabric go,
From the sewing room in Pittsburgh.
That no longer serves me.
Because the old fabric is no longer needed.
I'm weaving new fabric energetically.

I had the thought in the plane on the way to HQ,
All the skills that I had developed to be wife,
Particularly his wife,
Were no longer necessary.
And somehow that was comforting.
But letting go is hard.
Letting go of useless skills.
Things that are an obstacle to the new me.
Were so deeply engrained in the fabric of me.
So disguised that I don't recognize them,
It's all a bit confusing.
And the super planner can't figure out the next step.
If the house sells quickly,
I can take that step then.
After two or three people wanting the house,
And it not working out,
I'm in a quandary.
But as I feel into it,
I know it's all working perfectly behind the scenes.
And once again it's a message to let it go.
Romans 8: All things work perfectly.
Perfect.
Patiently.
Purging.
Weaving.
My meditation teacher says,

Everything happens in energy
Before you see it in physicality.
I set about to weave a new fabric,
A new energetic fabric of a new life.
It dawns on me, that the back and forth,
Of the shuttle when you weave,
Pendulates.

Co-worker Quandary

Not knowing what to say.
Not knowing how to say it.
Wanting to offer support.
But awkward,
Awkward silences.
Incompletely answered questions.
Like, "Why won't you go live near your sons?"
Me not wanting to open the wounds.
And holding back the water works.
Because "There's no crying at work, Delia."
(My favorite advice to my
Favorite sensitive emotional employee nurse.)
If he had died, there is a social protocol.
Flowers, cards, "sorry for your loss."
There is no social protocol for a separation.
There is no social protocol
For the depression that follows.
I say, "I'm back to writing,"
And them not really understanding the significance
Of returning to a single meaningful thing
That gives me joy.
How I get efficacy from writing.
Still avoiding all other activities
That were once meaningful.

I never even set up my sewing room.
I haven't finished a single needlework project
Since Christmas.
When reading isn't possible because I feel concussed.
How pulling my shit together
To show up for conference calls
Is a herculean effort.
All goes unspoken.
Because, honestly, they don't care in that way.
Who cares more about your shit than you do?
No one.
At least, that is what I thought back then.
I've learned differently now.
But back then, it was *no one else cares.*
And in a crowd of people,
I am once again alone.
But I have that crowd of people.
And I get to be around them again next week.

Chop Wood, Carry Water

I cook for one now.
Full meals whenever I am hungry.

My food budget goes muuuuuuuuch farther now.

I made meatloaf with raisin bread
And greatly enjoyed the hint of sweetness
That I would have been chastised for in the past.

My portions are still for a family of four.
Four is no more.
One is delightfully sufficient.

I savor every bite.
In perfect silence.
Free to be with my thoughts of how good the meal is.

Thanking God for food.
And being proud of my ability to nourish my body.
So that I can be here now.

Happy

Holier.
Awesome.
Peaceful.
Prosperous.
Yearning for a life of my own.
Happy.
I am learning to be happy in the now.
Alone.
I pledge my head to clearer thinking.
The first part of the 4-H pledge
Pops into my head from childhood.
My therapist says, "You are good with affirmations."
I am.
I am an affirmating, ass-kicking Mo' Fo'.
I crack me up.

From Wife to Life

I am free from the oppression of being married.
I am beginning to understand feminism from the inside out.
I am grateful for being free from the oppression of being wife.

I am non-wife.
I am history.
Allowing me to truly look forward to life, on my own.
Looking forward. Without my guard up.
No more blindsides. (Or so I thought.)

Free from criticism.
Free from constant negativity.
Free from exhalations that fill up the bedroom.
Until the alcohol in the air wakes me every day at 4:00 a.m.
Free from laundry that is so nasty it dries crunchy,
Stiff like a board.
Free to be.
Free to allow.
Free to have an uncensored life.
Free to experience.
All the sweetness
Life has to offer.

Being me,
Just me,
And I am grateful.

Passwords

I can't get into the online bank.
I panic.
I get extra security on my bank account.
I changed all my passwords.
I get the extra security from the credit agencies.
I get the extra security from Social Security.
The password for the RV was forgotten.
The reminder security question was:
Who is your best friend?
And my answer was
(Truthfully, this is what it was)
No one.
And I thought to myself
When I paid the second payment,
I gotta change that.
What frame of mind were you in
When you said
"No one" is your best friend?
Well, we know that's the harsh truth
But is that really serving you?
And my work password
Went from Lonewolf
To Risingstar.
And all the other passwords

Were changed to something
More uplifting.
More of an affirmation.
Because it's time to lift yourself up
By the password.
Multiple times a day.
Because
You are ascending.
Your star is rising.

Pittsburgh

"Hail to Pitt!"
I'm traveling back to the Burg,
Back to the land of the Yinzer.
I'm going to Giant Eagle to listen,
Listen more than to buy groceries,
To the native Pittsburgh tongue.
And to hear someone call someone
A jagoff.
I am suddenly
Very homesick.
I've nursed the homesickness
For two years and two months.
And it's time to know where to go
To relieve all the heartache
I've carried in my chest.
All the gut-wrenching pain
I've carried in my gut.
From the stupidest choice
I have ever made.
Rocky Point.
The rockiest point in my life.
Away from the Rocky Point.
You can never go backward.
But you *can* go where it's

Familiar.
And that is what I need right now.
Not "furmiliar,"
I say to everyone who mispronounces it.
Familiar.
Like family.
Like my son and his wife.
My family.
My support network.
My pastor.
My friends.
To see the Pens play.
To see Pitt Alumni.
And to be
Comforted by surroundings.
Where people know how to drive.
No North Carolina blinking yellow arrow.
When you need to turn left,
The traffic allows you to turn.
The Pittsburgh left turn.
Where people understand jagoff
Without explanation.
Where no one fucking blesses my heart.
I travel through the luminous light
Of a cloud.
And as the plane leaves Dallas,

I ascend at a rapid rate.
Like my rising star.
Like my mood.
Knowing that
I am not alone.
That my depression
Can come back.
But I summarily
Uninvite it to return.
I once issued a lifetime ban from my house
To a fourteen-year-old
Because of bad behavior.
I now banish my depression
From my brain.
I now banish sadness
From my heart.
I permit grief to run its course.
But sadness
That is like peanut butter stuck to my heart,
Can pick itself up,
And get out of my body.
For the first time
In a long time,
In Pittsburgh,
I choose me.
After denying myself,

In Pittsburgh,
Over and over,
Year upon year,
As I reflect on how,
I choose me.

Church

Three Sundays ago,
I get the whispering thought,
Go to church.
I missed the early service.
And again, the whisper,
Go to church.
I ready myself for the late service,
And I get dressed up.
Wear a skirt that is waaaay too big
Since I lost thirty pounds,
And I make myself presentable.
I read the lessons before church.
The entire service,
I kid you not,
Was about forgiveness.
Seventy-times-seven forgiveness*
And I weep like a baby
Through the whole service.
During the peace,
A grand Southern lady comes over
And hugs me.
I tell her I'm okay.
She says, "You're hurting."
I nod and say, "I'm strong."

And again, I kid you not,
She almost loses her Southern cool,
In church.
And her refined Southern drawl almost says,
"Strong is bullshit."
I see the words form in her mouth.
She realizes where we are.
Sometimes we feel vulnerable
In public,
And I swear I thought she was an angel.
Because I didn't see her the rest of the service.
So back to Sunday in Pittsburgh,
I promised both pastors that I would
Be in attendance.
In the most beautiful church
I have ever attended.
My church,
In Pittsburgh.
On Grant Street.
In the middle of downtown (said dahntahn).
I walked into
The Glory of God
On display at the
First English Evangelical Lutheran Church.
With nine angels up behind the altar,
Two angels on the left stained-glass window,

Two angels on the right stained-glass window,
And Jesus Christ sitting on the lap of his mother, Mary.
The Angels, Jesus, and Mary,
Right there in front of me.
I feel the glory of this holy place.
I read the lessons.
The entire first lesson,
I kid you not,
Had to do with planting
Over a long time,
And the fruit of all the effort resulted in wild grapes.
That you just had to let the wild grapes go.
"What more was there to do for my vineyard
That I have not done in it?"★★
And, wow, God is speaking to me.
God sees that I did it all. What more was there to do?
And it's time to let go.
The second lesson,
I kid you not, says,
Forget what lies behind
And strain forward to what lies ahead.★★★
Wow, God is really speaking to me.
And the third lesson,
Weaving in the planting and evil people
Who do despicable things.★★★★
The main Gospel lesson is how to handle rejection.

That it's not yours to mete out the justice.
That God sees it all.
This is God's world.
And I am just renting space and time.
And my heart begins to swell
As the best church choir *ever,*
Raises the vibration of the whole church.
And in my previously vacant heart,
I visualize a blue heart,
And I know my heart is filling,
Refilling with the love of God.
In that moment
I feel luminous.
I am not alone
In a crowd,
And I am connected
To my people
In Pittsburgh.

*Matthew 18:21-22
**Isaiah 5:4
***Philippians 3:13
****Matthew 21:33-43

Good Friends

Mary and Bob.
I text Mary that I'm going to be in town.
She says come after church.
She sends a text that she has prepared
A gluten-free lunch for me!
I arrive to see all her grandkids.
They all hug me.
I love every single one of them.
Although I do love the girls and the other boy,
A lot,
I love Jake the most.
Because he screams my name with delight
Every time he sees me.
And my heart fills.
I tell my long-standing friends,
Who I haven't seen in two years,
My tale of woe.
Because good friends
Will pick right back up
As if no time has elapsed.
And I love the lunch.
And I love the good conversation.
And I sit on her porch.
And realize that I am thinking more clearly,
More clearly than I have ever thought
In a very long time.

And I feel the shroud on my mood lift.
And I feel that God is not done with me yet.
And I watch the waterfall
That Bob so lovingly installed in the backyard.
And I relax.
I feel loved.
It's an interesting observation
On my part,
Almost clinical
To write this.
As I start to feel the depression wane,
I make up my mind.
I make up a new affirmation.
I'm going to stick around
To see what happens.
I feel strong.
I feel grace.
I feel connected.
I feel loved.
I feel alive.
I see myself thrive.
I am luminous.
I'm letting go of what no longer serves me.
I'm ready to kick depression's ass.
I am alive.
I am.
Lisa Schatz.

Triste

adj. sad, gloomy, desolate, dismal, sorry, sorry-looking

"Ella vivirá triste en esa isla."

She'll live sad on that island.

The Beach House

I begin looking for a place to live
Because I have to stay in NC
For a year,
According to NC divorce laws.
I hate this state, but let's make the best of it.
I search online and I find
Reasonably priced beach houses
In Onslow county.
Out on the north end of Topsail Island.
I search until I find
The unfurnished Volusia Drive home.
It's everything a beach house should be.
On stilts, it sways in strong gales.
Windows. Windows. Windows.
Ocean views from every window.
Intercoastal views from the rest.
Four balconies to step out and feel the breeze.
Hear the ocean.
I am in Onslow county.
On slow.
My life and the fever pitch of separating,
Selling Vogler's ten acres
And moving in,
Can finally slow down.
Until that knock on the door.

The very day that the check cleared from
Selling Rocky Point.
Just as I was taking a breather.
Feeling stronger.
Turning my heart forward to healing.
"Are you Lisa Schatz?"
Why did I open the door at night???
Papers thrust at me.
I take them.
Some jagoff in a pickup truck
Hands me papers.
And the peace I felt for six days evaporated.
It wasn't over.
I couldn't just wait out the year in peace.
I was being sued.
By a man who always thought everything was his.
Until it wasn't.
My first thought,
(And this is no lie),
May this lawsuit be for the highest good of all involved.
Loving-kindness.
It came to me when I needed it most,
And before I had the language to know what it was.
May this lawsuit be for the highest good of all involved.
And I lived close to that thought for eleven months.
In the beach house.

Fall on Your Knees

Christmas.
At the beach house.
I drive an hour to go to church.
And the stupid Southern church does not have services.
Because it was Sunday.
They did the Saturday night thing,
Even though I checked online.
That's when I got really mad at the Southern Lutherans.
Who does not have church on Christmas?!?
So, I did the next best thing.
I went shopping.
I went to Soma and bought righteous underwear.
I spent money on me.
Because I needed to feel good from the inside out.
You name it, I bought it.
I spent a lot of money on me.
Merry Christmas, Lisa.
Enjoy the matching sets, the bras, the thongs,
And toss out all those worn-out things,
Those threadbare things.
You don't have to skimp anymore.
Burn those matronly things
And step into the sexy crone you are.
Then I took a long walk on the beach.

Christmas at the beach is deserted,
So, I began to sing loudly
Because I did not get the chance at church.
Singing kid-embarrassingly loudly is my thing.
"The Pitt Alma Mater," "Hail to Pitt."
It's my thing.
And I started belting out "O Holy Night."
The wind and the waves
Carried away my voice
As fast as I sang it.
"*Fall on your knees,*
O hear the angel voices."
And at that point,
A huge wave crashed on the beach.
I hear it echo even now.
And I knew that God was there.
On the beach, and he heard my song.
I fell on my knees then,
Oshie licking the tears from my face.
And many, many times
Over the next eleven months,
I fell to my knees.
Heard the angel voices,
The angel voices that told me
I was not alone.

Shaky New Year!

The lawsuit shakes me to the core.
Back to not eating,
Not sleeping,
Déjà vu.
I revisit August's physiology in January.
Just the week before,
I meet with the lawyer.
Because I know my husband
Better than he knows himself.
And she says you have an iron-clad separation agreement.
I call her office the next morning,
After the knock on the door.
And, of course, they are on Christmas break.
A week goes by, and I'm stuck out on the island,
Because an ice storm turns the island into
A winter fairyland.
But Southerners can't drive in snow,
Much less ice,
So I have an online meeting with the attorney.
I have skills to work from anywhere.
She says, "Who's his attorney?"
And just to add drama to the story,
My attorney is already involved
In another lawsuit with his attorney.

My attorney says, "I know this attorney very well."
I google the other attorney upon the advice of counsel.
And there it is.
The type.
If you don't think men have a type,
I can give you incontrovertible confirmation.
Sandra Bullock's sister looked back at me
From the screen.
And so, it begins.

Camp Lejeune, the Marines, and Safety

Squadrons of pelicans patrol the beach.
Alternating.
Squadrons of helicopters patrol the beach.
Alternating.
Droning, day in, day out.
Marines are my neighbors.
Shirtless Marines jogging in the middle of winter.
Testosterone on testosterone.
Jacksonville, NC, has the highest number
Of unmarried men
In the entire US, according to the internet.
So, it must be true.
At every hour of the day,
There is a shirtless Marine jogging
Somewhere in the world.
Thank God for the shirtless Marine.
I understand what Madeline Kahn meant by,
"I love quicktime harch."
So, even though I live in fear of what might happen next,
I am surrounded by Marines
Who willingly put their lives on the line
For old ladies like me.
And, ladies, if you have to live in fear
For a year,
Go to North Topsail Beach.

It’s got to be the safest place
In the USA.
In the world.
And the views aren’t too bad either.
“I love quicktime harch.”

Suffering

Suffering is life,
Say the Buddhists.
What can you learn from the suffering?
Depression is suffering.
Becoming un-wife is suffering.
Unraveling all the skills
Used to stay in a marriage that is no more
Is suffering.
Immersed in daily reminders
Of a life that is no more.
Trying to build
A new life from scratch,
While in the midst of labor pains of letting an old life go.
Why couldn't he just let me go?
Why do I have to suffer through the unknown
Of what he has yet planned?
Wasting even more money on lawyers.
UUUUghchgh—the sound of disgust.
Waves crashing on the beach
Pull my attention out of my head, back to the now.
A winter storm, blowing frozen sand in my face
As I walk and walk and walk the beach.
Walking into my suffering.
Walking into my strength.

I will not crumble; I vow to myself.
I feel like crumbling.
I honor the feeling with walking and walking.
And with every mile on the sand,
I see the impermanence of life.
How the beach is different every single day
With every single tide.
And I see it as a metaphor of my life.
It will change.
And even the piece of concrete block
That stands by Beach Access 39
Gets weathered by the wind, the sand, and the waves.
The edges are worn smooth,
Yet it is clearly a concrete block.
I will change through this.
Edges worn smooth by wind, sand, waves.
Yet, like the concrete block, I will be the same.
My core essence is still in there.
And in that moment,
I assemble pieces of myself.
Once shattered,
Now coming back together,
Facing the winter storm.
Blowing fiercely in my face.
Head on.

Lady Nada

I tell the Reiki girl
About my walk, the storm,
Assembling pieces of myself.
She says, "You have powerful
Spirit guides who are helping you.
Lada Nada is assisting you."
She explains that Lady Nada heals
Sensitivity of the heart.
And leads the sincere seeker to
Mastery of emotions.
I have the desire,
The will to heal,
The strength to pursue
Healing by any means.
And I learn that the prayers
For help are being answered.
The Holy Spirit is sending
Helpers skilled in healing the wounded heart
To assist me with my walk.
I see flashes of gold and purple
As I go deep into the Reiki session.
I awaken from the session
Feeling calmer.
As I walk on the beach,

I look down to see
A beautiful gold and purple shell
Sent to me by Lada Nada from Atlantis.

Broken Glass

Eighteen.
I received eighteen crystal glasses as a wedding gift.
Ping! When you tap the side.
Ping all eighteen.
Do I even know eighteen people to invite them
To use these?
Eighteen shiny, hopeful glasses
That will fill up with liquid marriage.
Celebratory, but gone in an instant.
Eventually, one got dropped.
Most likely on that tile floor in the kitchen
Where everything broke, shattered, really.
You sweep it up.
But it's okay because there are seventeen more.
Over the years, more got dropped.
More shattered, one at a time.
More cleanup.
Cleaning up every time one broke.
There still were more.
It was okay.
Then the $35,000 bill to the IRS.
And a few more got dropped at the same time.
I went down on my knees to sweep it up,
But there were too many.

I had to keep going.
I crawled across broken glass,
Cut. Bleeding.
On hands and knees, I crawled.
Doing what I had to do.
Keeping it all together.
Glass in my hands, forearms, elbows,
Knees, and shins.
Keep going, the bleeding's not that bad.
Pick yourself up and walk.
Do what you have to do, Lisa.
Why is this glass minefield getting bigger?
Walking. Crying. Keep going.
I walked across broken glass when
I was left behind ostensibly to sell the Pittsburgh house.
He left in February. The house sold in September.
Me in Pittsburgh. Him in Wilmington.
Figuring out how to get the lawn mowed
Was the easiest part of being left behind.
Walking. Crying. Keep going.
It will all be okay.
I walked across broken glass when he cleared
A tiny portion of land and I lived in chaos.
Walking. Crying. Keep going.
I walked across broken glass, stopping only to pull
The occasional shard from my feet.

Just the big ones.
The little ones are of no consequence.
Walking. Crying. Keep going.
Do what you have to do, Lisa.
It will all be okay.
Then I stumbled.
I fell face down on the broken glass.
I fell hard. Stunningly hard.
My wits were knocked out of me.
The first thought I had was,
Keep going. Crawling. Crying.
As I lay shattered on the floor,
He perfunctorily says,
"You gotta do what makes you happy."
Really? After all I have done.
No extended hand. Just look away at the TV.
Well, that explains a lot.
Doing what I had to do, not what makes me happy.
Thanks a whole helluva lot.
Aloneness settles in.
As I lay shattered and bleeding on the floor,
In the bed of broken glass,
I looked up to see that it was him.
He was dropping all the glasses.
He was creating the bed of glass.
I am shocked to see this. Finally, and clearly.

I looked down.
I noticed a large shard of glass
In my chest;
I realized that it pierced my heart.
I felt the pain of a glass shard penetrate my heart.
I felt the pain of the glass shard shattering my heart
Into a million pieces.
No more keep going.
No more crawling.
No more tears.
I reached down to pull out the shard in my heart.
In the multifaceted crystal surfaces
There were the reflections of
All the faces of
All the women. "*We're just friends.*"
Younger, prettier, thinner, bubblier.
While I walked across broken glass.
The life that was shattered.
Little by little.
Crystal glass by crystal glass.
At first unintentional.
Then intentionally unintentional.
Until the minefield of broken glass
That I was willingly walking through daily
Pierced my heart.
And my heart shattered.

There was no way to reassemble
All that broken glass.
No more keep going.
No more crawling.
Crying.
Facedown, wondering,
What do I do now?
No more doing.
No more keep going.
Pick yourself up, Lisa.
Pivot and walk away.
Walk back to the sweetness of your innate nature.
It's there. You know it is.
With each soft step back
There will not be new wounds.
Pull out each shard and heal.
Every shard. Even the tiny slivers.
Walk on the soft sand.
Walk on the nurturing pre-glass sand.
Realize and recognize that it is much easier to walk on sand.
Walk softly on the shifting sand
That is your emotions.
Feel the internal shifts with
The changing tide.
Use the raw material of silica sand
To create the new vessel to hold your life.

To hold the fleeting liquid of life.
Be grateful for
No more broken glass.

Marine Pelican

The pelicans are hunting.
The pelicans are hungry.
Fly low and slow,
Then splash,
Head down, beak first
Like a cannonball.
Spying their breakfast.
Flying. Looking. Spying.
Diving. Solo hunting.
Not like the squadrons
In "V" formation that patrol the beach.
These are Oorah,
Semper Fi,
Mission-oriented,
Badass marine pelicans.
I watch from my beach chair as the tide creeps in.
In an instant, I connect with one.
I watch it fly deliberately.
I observe and watch it make attempt after attempt.
And the pelican succeeds.
And as it sits in the water,
Enjoying its successful breakfast,
Gulp,
It looks over at me.

We make eye contact.
I realize we are not unalike.
I learn that after many unsuccessful attempts,
If I am persistent, I will succeed.
The solo pelican provides for itself.
I should be like the solo pelican
That never wavers in its confidence
That it will provide for itself.
Is it the marine bravado?
Whatever it is, I learn from this solo pelican
That there are times to go it alone,
And times to get in that squadron and fly.
But to feed yourself,
Keep going.
Because success is inevitable.
Healing is inevitable.
You need to be like a badass marine pelican and
Go it alone.

The Cheese Stands Alone

I had my girl squad,
My lawyer, my therapist,
My Reiki girl, and the Reiki Shaman.
Count in the real estate agent, too.
But for all intents and purposes,
I was alone.
Alone with my thoughts.
Aloneness is like driving a golf cart
Full speed ahead over speed bumps.
There are no shock absorbers for aloneness.
As I drove over the high bridge
Linking Sneads Ferry to North Topsail,
I looked out at the sparkling ocean.
It's one of those heaven opening, angels singing,
"Waaaaaw" gorgeous moments
That takes your breath away.
The Ocean. The O Chin.
And at that moment of intense beauty,
I realized that
I had no one to share it with.
No one else to see the beauty of nature through my eyes.
Because,
The cheese stands alone.

The Blessings of the Beach House

Falling asleep to the sound of the tide changing.
Awakening to the sound of the tide changing.
Sitting in my office, looking out at the sparkling ocean.
Seeing dolphins playing during a work meeting.
Opening the screen doors to feel the breeze.
Walking Oshie on the sand.
Walking north to the end of the island.
Walking south to the Seaview Fishing Pier.
Walking, walking, walking.
Being away from the island
And dialing in to the pier webcam.
Getting "ooohs" and "aahs"
From workmates and customers.
"You live there??"
The island faces southward,
Tucked into the crescent beyond the elbow of the
Outer Banks.
I sit on the beach every chance I get.
I take my lunch to the beach.
The good negative ions wash over me
And help me release pent-up emotions.
I read with my beach chair in the water,
So the tide washes under my chair.
I get absorbed in the stories.

I read the healing treatise *True Refuge* by Tara Brach.
I read *All the Light We Cannot See* by Anthony Doerr.
I get so absorbed that I don't notice the tide coming in
And I get upended by a wave smashing into my chair.
More times than I care to admit.
Playing a trick on me
To learn mindfulness firsthand.
Pay attention to me, says the ocean.
The books are water-soaked and they dry crinkly.
Living at the ocean teaches you
About the impermanence of life
Every single day.
The tide changes. The shore changes.
When you vacation at the beach,
The impression of the beach on the days you were there
Sticks in your memory.
But it's a false memory.
Living there is an intense study in being in the moment.
The ocean changes the beach with every single tide.
If you walk in the morning,
You may walk through the detritus
Of shells I call Ocean Vomit.
Messy. Chipped. Disorganized.
You may walk along and suddenly
Have to step up two feet,
Because overnight, magically,

The shoreline eroded.
It may stay with that shelf for a week or so,
But then suddenly,
On the next walk,
The sand is smooth the whole way.
No more erosion shelf.
Where did it go?
Does it matter?
Lovely little tide pools emerge.
Fun to walk in.
You learn sand tolerance in a new way.
Don't wear tight flip-flops.
Walking will sandpaper your skin under the straps.
There is no hose at Beach Access 39.
You time the foot washing ritual
With the waves, and the dog pulling on the leash.
Except for the aforementioned shirtless Marine,
You are the only person on the beach.
The wind.
Another constant.
Fifteen miles per hour on calm days.
Every day.
I sit at my desk and I look out at the American Flag,
Flying high on the rental property down the way.
(Sadly, the flag did not survive Hurricane Florence.)
The wind is a force not to be ignored.

No sense in doing your hair.
It'll be blown to bits by the time
You take the ten steps to the car.
The wind reminds you
Of just how small and insignificant you are.
The tourists.
I once phoned the Jones-Onslow Electric Company
(JOEMC—I called them the Jag-Off Electric Company
Because you can't take the Pittsburgh out of the girl.)
To let them know that a kite had
Gotten loose and was flying from an electrical wire
Above my house.
From. An. Electrical. Wire.
Tourists.
We full-timers got your back.
The night before Florence hit,
We were told to evacuate the island.
The tourist renting the house next door,
Who kept using my water to wash himself,
Parked me in.
I went over at 8:00 p.m.,
Knocked and knocked and knocked.
He finally answered.
I asked him politely to move his car.
"You do know there is a hurricane coming,
And we have to leave tomorrow morning."

In typical, Southern, laid-back style,
He says, "Tomorrow will take care of tomorrow."
"Yes, sir. Please move your car.
I'm leaving first thing in the morning and
I can't drive the RV out with your car there."
Oy vey.
And as I drove off the island that
September morning, I felt
A profound sense of gratitude for
The solitude that started as
Aloneness.
But changed.
Radically changed.
Into a powerful awareness
Of profound gratitude
Of how my tiny life,
With my tiny problems
Like a specious lawsuit,
Were held by the vastness of the ocean
In great care,
While I sorted out
What came next.

Hurricane Florence

The island irrevocably changed.
I left on Tuesday.
I made it to Pittsburgh late Wednesday.
The storm hit Saturday night.
I watched the webcam until I couldn't.
I watched the weather channel.
The yellow house down the way
Was on the weather channel,
And I watched the garage doors
Get washed away.
Shock. Alarm. Hit me in the gut.
Maximum windspeed that kept increasing.
I "grounded" my house.
I put roots in that sucker that went to
The center of the earth.
Sadness, that the beauty
Of nature
Was being destroyed by nature.
The paradox did not escape me.
Over the course of several hours,
The sustained wind and water
Called "tide surge,"
Washed away the sixteen-foot-high dunes.
The dunes were gone.

I repeat, sixteen-foot-high dunes. Gone.
The Porta-Potty at Beach Access 39
Had sand up to the handle.
That's about four feet of sand washed inland.
The little dip in the backyard
Turned into a river.
With the Intercoastal at my back,
The water had an outlet.
The beachfront houses were trashed.
The North Topsail Beach Police
Took pictures of the destruction
Of the beachfront houses.
By pure happenstance,
There on the NTB Police Facebook page,
My house showed up
In the background of the picture.
And
It
Was
Safe.
Grounding and prayers work miracles.
I was evacuated for a month.
When I went back,
In my haste to leave,
I dropped a receipt
In the entrance.

The receipt was dry.
Untouched.
Not a drop of water in my house.
Across the way,
Not a drop in the Marine's house.
We full-timers were spared.
And when I returned,
The Penguins flag
That I hung in celebration
On the house
When I moved in
Was still there.
Tattered, but strongly attached
To the beach house
That withstood the hurricane.
I took it as a sign that
I was fine.
Everything was going to be fine.
Fast forward, that Penguins flag
Hangs by my pool in my new house.
Every time I see it,
It is a tangible reminder that
I can withstand the chaos of the hurricane
Of my life,
And live to tell the tale.

Should I Stay or Should I Go?

I loved that beach house.
I wondered, Could I swing it?
Could I buy it?
The hurricane put the kibosh on that.
At high tide
On the full moon,
The ocean came across
The tiny little road,
My only access road,
And covered it with feet of water.
I was essentially marooned
On an island.
With all my stuff.
Florida it is.
Flo-Ri-DAH.
People. Civilization.
And my mood brightened.
My Florida realtor
Would send me pictures of houses
Everyday.
And I would look at them.
I narrowed my choices.
Pool. Two story.
Gas range.

Lots of natural light.
I scanned the emails every day.
But living with the unknown,
When would NC be over,
Was unmaking all the planning.
Live in the now.
The end of the marriage is not yet.
The new life is not yet.
Not. Yet.
Liminal, once again.

Show Me Your Papers

The divorce was filed 367 days
After the separation.
The absolute soonest day
That I could do it.
August 14, 2018.
Then, the hurricane.
After I got back,
I called the deputy who was
To serve the papers.
They had sixty days. To serve.
Sixty days.
Not served yet.
Yet—that liminal YET.
On October second, I call.
Voicemail, again.
I think that he thinks I am going to chew him out.
The deputy, that is.
So, I send loving-kindness to him.
The voice message I leave:
"Sir, I know you are doing your level best.
You need to go to his address before 8:00 a.m. or after
10:00 p.m. at night."
The next morning,
A call from Deputy Southern Drawl.

"Ma'am, the papers were served at 6:15 a.m.
This morning."
The end of the marriage is not yet.
The new life is not yet.
Not. Yet.
But this time it's on its way.
Thank you, Deputy Southern Drawl.

Another Trip Around the Sun

Sixty.
Sixty trips around the sun.
Three funerals in ten months.
First it was Dad.
He was nearly ninety,
Was suffering from memory loss,
Was treated unkindly by my mom.
She was an incapable caregiver from way back.
He checked out.
Aunt Audrey came and held his hand.
Audrey sat with Dad as he transitioned to the afterlife.
I reconnected for the first time
With Audrey and her family,
With Audrey's daughters,
At Dad's funeral.
Then it was Audrey.
She had cancer.
She was eight years older than me.
Twenty-three years younger than Dad.
I took that one hard.
Her family took that one hard.
She turned out to be a great mom.
Then it was Uncle Buck's wife.
She had cancer too.

And through all that sadness,
And trips back to Pittsburgh,
I told my cousins,
"I'm turning sixty and I'm throwing a party.
Enough sadness.
Let's have some fun."
Rental Hall in the West End.
Beach-themed decorations.
Beach towels from
The Shark Attack Gift Shop, a local landmark,
As party favors.
(Google *Shark Attack Sneads Ferry* to see it.
You walk in a shark's mouth to get to the door).
Caterer who does gluten-free.
DJ who plays sixty-year-old-type dance music.
I decided to wear sequins.
Sequins mean something to me.
I wore sequins in high school.
I wore sequins in college.
I was a majorette.
Sequins take me back to my youth.
I put the dress on and thought,
I feel really good in sequins.
Why don't I wear them more often?
"NO gifts," I say.
"I'm moving and I don't want to take more stuff.

Just cards.
A card contest.
"Who can make me laugh?" I say.
And they went all out.
Of course, Diana went over the top,
Exceeding all my expectations
With a handmade card that lit up!
Cousin Natalie had the funniest card.
A little naughty but hilarious.
Friends.
Every single person who meant something
Showed up.
Including Cathy, who was my first patient.
She told me at yet another funeral
That she uses the beach towel
Every morning when she gets dressed.
We danced.
We sang.
We had a high-octane sugary birthday cake.
Billy helped me take pictures.
Pictures of me with everyone.
Dawn, Diana, Paul, Olivia,
Mary, Bob, Jill, Abby,
Katy, Baby Nora,
David, Liz, Jane,
Eddie, Kim,

Billy,
Natalie, Mike, and Gina,
Laura, Mike, and their three boys,
Garrett, Gavin, and Joshua,
Rebecca,
Cathy.
People who loved me enough to show up.
And as the night wrapped up,
I briefly thought back to
"You are never alone,"
To those two dark days.
This party was a milestone party, yes,
But a significant milestone in measuring
How far I've come.
I acknowledged how much progress I'd made.
And I knew that I was being held
In the thoughts of friends,
Who have become family,
Who are never more than a Facebook away.
Social proof
That I matter to some.
That night,
The cheese did not stand alone.

Courtroom Drama

Me trying to explain it to my friend:
Me: There are the divorce proceedings,
Which won't happen until November thirtieth.
Her: You filed in August,
And it won't be heard until November?
Me: Yes, November thirtieth, to be precise.
Her: What is taking so long?
Me: It's North Carolina.
Her: Remind me never to move there.
Me: That's only half of it.
Her: What do you mean?
Me: Well, there is still that lawsuit.
Her: What lawsuit??
Me: I'm sure I told you he is suing me.
I got the papers right after Christmas.
Her: So, there are two legal proceedings?
Me: Yes, one in Pender County,
One in New Hanover. And I live in Onslow County.
Everything here is On Slow.
Her: How are you holding up?
This has to be stressful.
Me: You have no idea.
Everything they need,
Information—they call it discovery—

Opens the wound again,
Because I have to see
How many phone calls he made
To other women.
How much money he spent in bars.
Her: OMG, I cannot believe you
Aren't curling up right now.
Me: Here is how I'm handling this:
I get a piece of paper.
I draw the courtroom from memory
From the first time I was there
Last July.
I google *Judge Faison.*
I read everything I can about him.
I draw his bench on the picture.
I draw me and my attorney.
I draw him and his attorney.
I don't draw well, so it looks
Like a primitive Marc Chagall,
Complete with curved arms.
(I take out the dog-eared well-worn picture.)
Here is what I do with this picture,
I go one by one around the courtroom,
I picture each person in my mind,
I take my time and say to them,
"May this proceeding be for the highest good

For all involved."
I do that for every single person—
The judge,
The clerk,
My attorney, his attorney,
Me, him.
(Note to reader:
Before I was trained in loving-kindness,
Before I knew what it was and the impact,
I came up with this way to handle this situation.
The power of loving-kindness
Helped me through the most stressful,
Contentious situation of my life,
And it paid off.)
Her: You are way more evolved than I am.
I am so pissed at him for you.
Me: You are a good friend,
But that won't objectively help for me to hold that.
I've got to let that go.
There is a chance that I lose,
That I have to pay,
That I have to come up with a chunk of money,
To add **that** insult to all this injury.
Then I would pay his court **and** attorney fees.
Her: OMG, Lisa, when is this going to end?
Me: Exactly.

I am stuck in the damn liminal phase.
Again.

Two weeks later:
My attorney: Your ex's attorney has filed a motion
To get off his case and quit being his attorney.
Me: You've got to be kidding me.
I already know why without you telling me.
He quit paying her.
Her: Yep. You're right.
Me: Where does that leave me?
We will have to start all over with a new attorney.
When? Why? This is torture.
Her: Hang tight, I have an idea.
We have a court date for this on December third.
Me: Okay, I think I can talk to my boss and get it off.
Her: I'm going to handle this.
You don't have to go.
I got this.

Fast forward to Friday, November thirtieth:
10:01 a.m., the phone rings.
I look, it's my attorney.
I answer.
She says: Congratulations, Lisa Nezneski.
Your divorce is final.

Me: Oh, thank you. Do you have the notarized copy?
Her: Yes. You can pick it up today.
Me: What about the other matter?
Her: It's Monday.
I got this.
And Miranda Lambert sings,
"Got My Name Changed Back."
Weekend of Numb.
Have you ever felt numb?
Really numbed out?
Like a thick fog is around your brain?
That you can't see anything
In front of you?
That your own hand
Is that my hand?
Is unfamiliar.
I went through two more days
Of intense numbness.
You would think
That, after two years of separation,
365+2 days of filing for divorce
And over ninety days more,
I would be glad it was over.
You would think.
But, no, it was a numbing fog.
Did I eat today?

Oshie, did I feed you?
A profound disconnection
Permeated my entire being.
Unfeeling.
No. Feelings.
Wandering
Mindlessly.
That was the most
Anti-mindful period of this entire transition.
Until Monday arrives,
I do as my attorney says.
I go about my life as I know it.
At 10:06 a.m., the phone rings.
It's my attorney.
I answer.
Her: Lisa, are you willing to settle the lawsuit?
Me: Yes, I am, but what does that mean, exactly?
Her: I am going to get the lawsuit dismissed
With prejudice.
That means he cannot come back and sue again.
Me: *Silence. Incredulousness.*
Her: Lisa, did you hear me?
I am moving to get his suit dismissed.
You get the timeshares. He doesn't want them.
He will sign that paper to the DMV.
Now, if you settle,

You cannot get your court fees
Or my fees paid by him.
You would be entitled to that
If we continue and you win.
I've been telling you all along
You will win.
Me: I am done.
If it means that he cannot come back
And sue again,
That I will finally be done,
Do it.
Get the lawsuit dismissed.
We hang up.
I am in a two-hour meeting.
I put all of this out of my head.
I have to be present
To be effective at my job.
The meeting lasts the whole two hours.
It ends at 12:02 p.m.
AT 12:12 p.m., the phone rings.
Me: Hello, Janet.
Her: Lisa, your suit is dismissed with prejudice.
You can pick up the signed and notarized copies
In the office later today.
Me: Tomorrow is soon enough.
Janet, is it really over?

Her: Yes, Lisa. It is finally over.
So, in the span of four days,
Two lousy years of marking time,
Being in a liminal period
Is over.
It. Is. Finally. Finally. Over.
Now to pack up and move out of this state.

The Year of Intense Healing

I lived in the beach house
For thirteen months
Or thereabouts—minus the hurricane evacuation.
Healing takes place
Every day.
Tempered joy.
Cautious optimism.
Isolation and aloneness.
Turns to peaceful solitude.
And my emotional range grew.
I forgave.
A lot.
Often.
I did not want to carry anything forward.
I prayed.
A lot.
Often.
Prayers for guidance, wisdom, understanding.
I let things go.
I made fifteen trips to Goodwill.
Clothes.
Household goods.
Books.
Miscellaneous equipment.

I let a lot of things go.
I sold, donated, and Marie Kondo-ed my life.
With every step I walked on the beach,
I gained perspective.
Insight.
Funny how the mindfulness training is "insight."
Vipassanā.
I was drawn to mindfulness
Like a moth to a flame.
I meditated every single day.
Morning, night.
During breaks.
Mindful walks on the beach.
Insights came during so many of those walks.
Notes in my phone.
I kept up with therapy, Reiki.
Intense self-care.
Louise Hay's mirror work.
Debbie Ford's shadow work.
James Van Praagh Spiritual Healer course.
I came out of that year
Stronger,
More in tune with my emotional weather.
And resilient.
Poems began to pour out of me.
I came to know myself better.

With a daily writing practice,
I challenged beliefs.
I challenged old and new beliefs.
I challenged myself to think in new ways.
I challenged everything.
In essence, during that prolonged
Liminal phase,
I was creating,
I was creating my life anew.
I made new observations about myself:
I like sleeping alone.
I **really** like sleeping alone.
I am quite capable
Of repairing all the damage
Created from inattention to myself.
I can pay attention to detail at work.
No question.
But do I check in with Lisa?
Do I tune in to how a conversation makes me feel?
Do I know what to do with those feelings?
I am learning.
Do I tune in to this vessel
That everyone calls Lisa?
My body. It's my ride.
I've got to stick with the one who brought me.
Pacing myself.

Honoring tiredness.
Understanding that exhaustion
Will take years to repair.
Being gentle.
Be gentle with yourself.
Be gentle with others.
Respect your intuition.
Acknowledge all the miraculous things
That have happened
While living at the beach house.
Healing is a process
Full of two steps forward,
One back.
A pendulation between
Forward motion,
Regression,
Relationship recidivism,
And release.
Healing your emotional life
Is like excavating a long-lost civilization.
It's been there
The whole time
But you didn't recognize it.
Or if you knew it,
You didn't acknowledge it.
And it is full of wonderment.

Of gazing inwardly to
Your source of truth.
The sense of being
On the right path.
Even if the path winds around
Like the chambered nautilus.
The Fibonacci sequence.
Each time you return
To the same place as before,
You are at a higher level,
With more understanding,
More compassion,
More wisdom.
And that is what
I've learned from
The Year of Intense Healing.
Wisdom is imparted
From the meaning
We gain from
The experiences
Held deeply
Within our bodies.
Wisdom connects us
With our souls.

Augenblick

n. (lit.) *"in the blink of an eye,"* a "decisive moment in time" that is fleeting, yet momentarily eventful and incredibly significant.

Luminous

I flew through a cloud today,
Immersed in the light of heaven.
White light above, below, all around,
Reflecting.
Immersed in the light of heaven.
Turbulence. Turbulence wakes me from the reverie.
The shaking proves that it is not solid,
An illusory temporal experience of the
Light of the afterlife.
And emerging from the cloud, a city appeared,
Placed down on terra firma.
The destination is ahead.
Billions of people scurrying around.
What if they were all suddenly mindful
And looked up
To see the luminous light of heaven
Inside a cloud?

Backstory on "Luminous"
May 8, 2017

I was on an American Airlines flight from Wilmington, NC, to Philadelphia, PA, traveling to attend the Wharton School for Executive Education. I was reading a book by Linda Metcalf on proprioceptive writing, and, suddenly, the plane was immersed in the brightest cloud I had ever seen. I was sitting in a window seat, and I was compelled to stop reading and look out to enjoy the moment. This entire poem was composed—uploaded, really—into my head in minutes.

Pack 'Em Up, Move 'Em Out

Seventeen days.
Thank God it was December,
When work slows down.
In seventeen days,
I packed up my whole house,
Sold all my furniture.
Rented a twenty-three-foot U-Haul
And got the hell out of Dodge.
It went down like this:
First, rent the U-Haul
At the closest place off the island.
Ask the U-Haul guys for a "moving guy."
They recommend this guy,
A former Marine (no kidding),
Who came in and took charge.
He had me take pictures of the furniture.
He posted the ads.
He fielded the calls.
He set the price and got a cut.
I got what I wanted,
He got what he wanted.
Transactional relationship.
The rest of the furniture
I sold to Miss Carla's.

Carla sold me the sofa
And the table where I sat and wrote every morning.
Carla helped me figure out
How to turn the rocking horse
Into a unicorn for the baby.
Carla generously bought it all back.
The sofa, the table, the bedroom,
The end tables, and anything else
I wanted to sell.
All the while I'm working full time.
I know I want to go to Kissimmee.
I call around and find a "CubeSmart."
CubeSmart looks really nice in Hampstead,
And there is a brand-new CubeSmart in Robinson in Pittsburgh.
I look for Irlo Bronson Memorial Highway,
Which, in my many trips to Orlando,
Stuck in my head as the main drag.
East Irlo is way the hell out there.
But what do I know?
I arrange to store my stuff at CubeSmart.
I arrange to have my mail sent to
Mail Express—West Irlo Bronson,
Way the hell in the OTHER direction.
But what did I know?
Irlo is Irlo, right?

Moving Day.
"Is the U-Haul in Sneads Ferry where I rented it?"
"Why, no, ma'am, it's in Jacksonville."
Jacksonville.
So, I call the Marine Dude and he comes with me.
He drives me there.
He inspects the U-Haul.
Thank God for the Marines.
Marine shows up on moving day with two dudes.
They pack that U-Haul all day.
Let me explain the beach house:
First floor is just a lobby with a staircase.
The second floor is full of bedrooms.
One was an office,
One was the master bedroom,
One was full of boxes that I never unpacked.
Eighteen steps up, turn eight steps
To the second-floor landing.
Then up to the third floor.
Eight steps up to the landing,
Turn, up eight more steps to the third floor.
All day the three dudes go up, turn, up.
Down, turn, down.
Washer down. Dryer down.
The unit's washer-dryer combo back up.
Boxes. Totes. Boxes.

The kitchen table with six chairs.
The sewing desk.
Meanwhile, it dawns on me,
Where am I going to live?
I was so preoccupied with the going,
I forgot about the destination.
Where am I ending up?
And that it was December. Christmas.
I forgot about snowbirds
Who go to Florida in the winter.
I'm looking online.
No availability in Orlando until February.
No availability in Cocoa. Ever.
No availability in Tampa.
I call the Thousand Trails people.
I say, "Give me anything in Florida."
They give me Clermont.
Okay, whew, Clermont.
And where exactly is Clermont?
Central Florida.
North of Orlando.
Okay, north is good.
And that is settled for the first month.
Now to pack up the RV
While Marine and Two Dudes are finishing up.
They worked their asses off

Up and down the Fibonacci spiral of the stairs.
I start loading the RV with stuff that can be loaded.
I leave the rest for later.
I fall, exhausted, onto the blow-up bed.
Oshie's looking at me,
What happened to our bed, Mom?
And I sleep the sleep of exhaustion.
The next morning,
Oshie goes to the Dawg Farm.
And I drive as far as Savannah.
I stay overnight.
I get up the next day,
I haul ass to meet the movers I hire on the other end.
And I am at East Irlo Bronson by noon.
Two Men and a Truck show up.
Do you see a theme here?
And for the rest of that day,
The U-Haul is unpacked, and stuff is put into storage.
I made no further plans than to get there (again).
I see a U-Haul return place next door.
I call U-Haul and I tell them
I'm taking the U-Haul next door.
By this time, it's dark.
I call Uber to take me to the airport.
I splurged on a very expensive hotel room at the
Orlando airport.

I wish I could have enjoyed it.
By the time I got there,
I had less than six hours until my flight.
Next morning, I fly back to Wilmington.
Take an Uber to the Dawg Farm.
I call another Uber to take me back to the beach house.
Uber shows up and says,
"I'm not taking a fucking dog in my car."
Why does everything in NC have to be this hard?
Why are these people so difficult?
I'm exhausted.
I call another Uber.
He is a gentleman.
He takes me and Oshie home.
He is happy to get the long fare.
And then more flurry of activity.
Packing the RV.
Putting the car on the tow dolly.
Everything but the fridge.
I'll do that in the morning.
That RV was packed with all the pictures
That hung on the wall.
The lamps.
The sewing machines.
And totes of what I thought I would need to live
In the RV.

Twenty-three feet long by twelve feet wide.
Packed floor to ceiling with things
That I thought were breakable.
I would take responsibility
For all the breakables.
The last thing I do before I pull out of Volusia Drive
Is take a bath. One last luxurious bath.
Who knows how long it will be
Until I can actually get into a tub and bathe?
I say goodbye to the O Chin one last time
With a longish walk with Oshie, and
I'm off.
The Flo-Ri-Dah adventure begins.
That night, I had to move a picture to
Lie on the bed to sleep.
Halfway there, Savannah.
I google a Walmart or was it a Sam's?
I sleep overnight in the Walmart parking lot.
When I hit Flo-Ri-Dah on I-95,
I honked my horn and I whooped.
Oshie looks over at me from her co-pilot basket
Like what is wrong with you now?
I sing along with the Pistol Annies.
"Got My Name Changed Back."
Sometime around noon,
On the twenty-third of December, I reach Clermont.

Seventeen days.
Seventeen days of doing.
I put all my emotions on hold,
Because the driving emotion
Was to get out.
Leave.
Leave it all behind me.
I'm done. So be done.
After 499 days,
August 11, 2017 to December 23, 2018,
It's really over.
I really can begin anew.
And for the next week,
I sleep the dreamless sleep
Of profound adrenal exhaustion.
I don't have the strength
To celebrate.

House Hunting

Christmas Day, I wake up,
And still in bed,
I open my email.
Incredibly,
The very house that I took
A snip of in November,
And named the file "My New House,"
Was back on the market.
On Christmas.
It was a clear sign
That I interpreted.
Let's get settled, Lisa.
Merry Christmas to me.
Magical things started happening
Every day after Christmas.
Was it because I was so near to Hogwarts?
I call the realtor the next day.
We go see it.
She arranges to see about ten houses that day.
My hopes are dashed.
It's ugly, run-down,
Way more work than I can muster.
She arranges to see every pool house
In the greater Orlando area.

Over the next three days,
We use Waze and a masterful
Route to see the entire
Universe of pool houses.
She finds a house like the Christmas house.
But better.
8765.
We pull into 8765.
I hear a voice say,
"You're home."
I get the hit in my gut.
Home.
We go inside.
Natural light.
Tons of natural light.
Gas range.
Laundry room.
Big bathtub.
Pool.
It has everything.
The realtor and I drop off Oshie at the Dawg Farm.
I fly out for work the next day.
8765 is stuck in my head.

Weekend at Nancy's

Denver in January.
Who schedules these projects?
I stay at the Brown Palace.
I stay in a Princess Hotel.
We work hard for four days.
No way am I flying back to Orlando
Just to be back on Monday.
I'm stepping out of my comfort zone.
I'm going to stay with someone
I have never met in person.
We have taken classes together.
She offered.
I thought, Why not?
What's the worst that can happen?
It was wonderful.
We gelled a true friendship
That weekend.
We truly had a mystical weekend.
I stayed in a private suite
In her house.
And the bed welcomed my road-weary bones.
The house had fabulous energy.
It lifted my mood tremendously.
Meanwhile, I tell the realtor to

Make a bid on 8765.
On Saturday, I received a text.
They accepted my offer.
I'm buying a house!
I have a place!
No snakes, no bears.
Sunlight.
Rich, welcoming Florida sunlight.
My mood soars.
We went to the bookstore,
I found books that spoke
To my deep desire to heal.
We went to Whole Foods for dinner.
We girlfriend-talked for hours.
I find a kindred spirit in Nancy.
Sunday is Graduation Day!!
We go to Psychic Horizons,
And during the church service,
Nancy and I are ordained.
We become ordained ministers
Of the Church of Inner Light,
Boulder, Colorado.
After months and months
Of live, remote classes,
Nancy and I arrive at the seminary,
Meet all the wonderful teachers.

We talk about grounding the
Beach house during the hurricane.
It was a story they liked to tell.
Grounding was a technique they taught me.
They take credit.
I give them credit.
They were with me during every difficult step of the last six months.
Such positive and good energy here.
Nancy and I leave on a good-vibes high.
She says, "Have you seen *On the Basis of Sex*?"
I must have had a look on my face.
She says, "The Ruth Bader Ginsburg movie."
I say, "No, but this is the weekend to step out of my comfort zone.
The only thing I know about Ruth is that
She was a majorette—like me."
We go.
I am transfixed.
She, Ruth, is an amazing person.
I feel jealous that she encouraged her daughter
To see Gloria Steinem.
I adopt her.
I adopt her spirit as a strong woman.
I adopt her spirit as a mother figure.
An accomplished working mother figure.

Afterwards, I say to Nancy,
"You know that my granddaughter
Will be born in the next two days or so."
Nancy looks over with disbelief.
She says, "It's another sign."
I say, "I know."
So, the magic of the weekend
Stayed with me.
A week later, I hear Justice Ginsburg
Is unwell.
I write to her.
The address online.
Justice Ginsburg, Supreme Court of the United States.
I tell her how much I admire her.
I tell her how much the movie changed and transfixed me.
I send her loving-kindness to be well.
I stay at Nancy's until Monday,
And then drive over to work.
I get that call.
It's my son.
He says, "We are headed to the hospital.
My wife is in labor
With your granddaughter."

My Granddaughter

My granddaughter is on her way.
She is to be named after her great-grandmothers.
Strong female role models.
A female offspring.
One-fourth of her is me.
I will cultivate
Every good thing of me
And bring it out in her.
She is 25 percent Lisa,
100 percent her own person.
She is a tranquil, serene child.
Unlike her father.
She does not cry continuously.
A befuddled young mother with no support
For a crying baby
Is not my son or his wife's experience.
My prayers are answered.
A granddaughter.
I prayed the entire time of your labor to enter the world.
I called upon Mother Mary, Kuan Yin, Lady Nada, Eve.
I pray my heart out.
I welcome my spirit guides.
I call on her mother's spirit guides.
I call on Eddie's spirit guides.

I ask for the baby to have spirit guides.
I ask that generations and generations of ancestors
Surround the birth bed of the baby
And support her and her mother
In this transition to independent life.
It is 3:33 a.m. Colorado time.
I awaken. I think it has to have happened.
An hour later,
I get the call that my granddaughter came into the world
At the precise moment of my awakening.
A sign.
A sign that we are profoundly connected,
Which is what I've been praying for since May.
That this child has a connection to me.
Augenblick.
Augenblick indeed.

8765 Is Real on February 22

"The mortgage broker says when?
When do you want to close on this house?"
I say, "February 22,
And it would be great if we could schedule it for 2:00 p.m."
Done.
On February 22, by the time I get to
The actual signature part,
It's 2/22 at 2:22 p.m.
From the Angel Numbers website:
"*Number 222 has to do with balance,*
Manifesting miracles
And new, auspicious, and timely opportunities.
Angel Number 222 encourages you
To take a balanced, harmonious, and peaceful stance
In all areas of your life.
The message is to keep the faith
And stand strong in your personal truths."
Liminal is really over this time.
8765 is a manifested miracle.
I have arrived.
Augenblick.

Two Steps Forward, One Step Back

That Friday night,
I move into the house. My house.
I move the RV to the driveway.
I move the food to the fridge.
I blow up the blow-up bed.
(That f'in thing has come in so handy,
Time and time again.)
At 8:00 p.m., I fall into a deep sleep.
RAP RAP RAP.
What, where am I?
RAP RAP RAP.
RAP RAP RAP.
Where are my clothes?
What is going on?
Nebby Debbie (a Pittsburgh term for nosy neighbor)
Is knocking.
She proclaims with great authority,
"You can't park that RV there."
I say, "How is that any of your business?"
She says, "Well, you are going to get a ticket."
I say, "I can afford a ticket."
She: "Well, you better move it."
I reiterate: "It's none of your concern.
Now, goodnight."

I close the door
And start to shake.
Did I make a mistake?
Why in the world would Nebby Debbie stick her nose in?
Forget it, Lisa.
Go back to bed.
The next morning,
I decide to get rid of the lentils.
I put them down the disposal.
BAD IDEA.
Never put lentils down the garbage disposal.
I tried a plunger.
Nothing.
I call Roto-Rooter.
Hippolyte comes on Monday.
I can't make this up;
The Roto-Rooter man is named Hippolyte.
He tells me to never put starchy things down the drain.
He says my drain was clogged
Between the house and the street.
Didn't I have an inspection?
Well, yes, Hippolyte, I did,
But I guess they didn't check that.
Later that day,
I start to put dishes away.
I open the cupboard to see

The cupboard was already occupied.
The old occupants went scurrying
When they saw the new occupant.
Oy vey. German cockroaches.
The bug man at the beach house educated me on the art
Of cockroach identification.
I stopped putting everything away.
I knew that I would have to remove everything
From the cupboards
To appropriately treat the German variety
Of cockroaches.
The "bad" variety.
Again, I say, Oy vey.
Later that Monday,
11:00a.m., Jose comes to spray for bugs.
I'm outside with Oshie.
Jose pulls up and I greet him.
As we are talking,
A swarm of bugs engulfs us.
I say, "This wasn't here earlier.
This just happened."
I say, "What kind of bug is this?"
Thinking it's a no-see-um or some other native
Floridian insect.
Nope.
He says, "Ma'am, you have termites."

T.E.R.M.I.T.E.S.
Didn't you have an inspection?
Why, yes, I did, as a matter of fact.
Inspection Man is rude, not helpful, and "sorry, ma'am,
But my services are complete."
Termite treatment:
Spraying, outdoor thingies.
Jose in the attic.
A week later,
I'm standing, working at the kitchen counter.
I feel something touch my leg.
I think it's Oshie.
I look up and she is across the room.
I look down.
Scene from a horror movie.
My legs are covered with
T.E.R.M.I.T.E.S.
Walls were ripped out.
Outdoor wood was ripped off the house,
Replaced with stucco
By the businessman, Stucco R US,
With questionable practices
And poor communication.
(He tells me, "My wife died." I feel sorry.
Later, I google him. The wife died three years ago.)
He never finished the painting.

Now I need to rent a ladder
And paint exposed stucco—I digress.
So, Jose fixes me up.
I get the termite bond,
Ostensibly to protect me in the future.
I certainly hope so.
The Reiki girls tell me
That the house is purging.
The house is purging all the bad energy.
The house is letting go of all low vibrations
To match me.
I go with that.
I set up the meditation room.
The room is my second office
Where my personal business,
Healthy Mindful Self,
Is located.
Healthy Self was in Sewickley.
The happiest job I ever had.
I'm coming back to what was, only better.
Healthy Mindful Self.
The new venture.
I imbued nothing but good vibes throughout the house.
Meditation twice daily.
Sage.
Palo Santo.

I have a second office,
Or is it the first?
For all my day job work.
Two distinct areas,
Two distinct endeavors,
With enough space.
I am grateful
That if the termites with a capital T had to be here,
They popped out at the exact second
Jose showed up.
I am grateful
That I have enough space.
After living for two months in
Less than 300 square feet,
I am now in nearly 10x.
I get it.
I have 10x-ed my life.
Two steps forward,
One tiny, dealt-with step back.
Note to self: Never put lentils down the disposal.

Should I Do It? Toe in the Water

You know, join a dating site.
The girl squad all say, "It's time, Lisa."
I'm like, "I don't know."
I think about my editor,
Who has sworn off dating.
She is raising her daughter.
That is her priority.
I admire her. I would have done the same.
I did do the same. Sort of.
The Reiki girls say,
"We get a strong hit that you should do
SilverSingles."
I am running errands out to Home Depot
For yet another happy homeowner piece of equipment.
On the drive, I hear a text noise.
At the red light, I look.
A message on Meetup?
I didn't know you could private message on Meetup.
It's a really handsome guy who wants to know if I'm single.
So, we text for a bit.
And I think, Okay, it's time.
I'm floating in my pool
With one toe in the water,
On the giant unicorn float,

Because why not?
And on impulse,
I join SilverSingles.
Meetup guy turns out to be one of those
Russian love scammers.
What do they say about toads and princes?
I get a text:
Do you like to kiss?
I'm like, WTF?
It gets worse,
I say buh-bye.
I block, or something.
Whatever.
I head up to Pittsburgh
For my granddaughter's Christening.
It's Sunday.
I'm emotional about the Christening.
I'm trying to explain why I'm emotional
To the Meetup guy.
He sends me this long, flowery poem.
I'm like, Okay, antennae up.
This sounds nothing like this guy.
I take the poem and I copy/paste into Google.
It's some love poem
Written by a high school sophomore.
Okay.

I tell him: *I see that this poem*
Was written by someone else.
I say: *You know I'm a writer.*
I say: *You should have given credit*
To the high school sophomore
Who wrote it.
He ignores that.
He does it again, someone else's work.
Passed off as his own.
I say buh-bye.
I get a text from Rolando.
Interesting. Handsome. Friendly.
He asks how I am on the rainy morning in Orlando.
I say: *I'm not home.*
I say: *I'm at the baby's Christening.*
I'll be back later that day.
He is kind.
He is for reals.
His number checks out on Spy Dialer.
Everything he tells me checks out on BeenVerified.
He likes to dance.
He has a beard.
We go out on a date.

No Ordinary Day

I stood at my bedroom window this morning
And watched the sun rise.
I watched as the light expanded
And pastel Florida colors reflected off the clouds.
I lost track of time watching the high wispy clouds
That shimmered with radiant light.

As the curtain of night lifted,
I heard a bird in the tree below welcome me to the day,
Inviting me to the fullness of all that will be.
This day is different.

Not like all the other ordinary days
That are linked together by sameness,
Like the sameness in a string of perfect pearls.
This day sparkles.
This day is like a precious gem.

Moments before, from my bed,
I discovered that overnight
I was sent a love poem
By Rumi.

I listened to Rumi and his beloved pledge their love,
A holy love.
And with that glorious way to start the day,
I knew this day was different.

Days slip by like the passing of rosary beads
Through your fingers.
Like prayers said with mindless rote repetition
Without thought to the meaning or content.

This day is not to slip by.
This day is different.

My life has been trials, tribulations, and uncertainty,
And yet I go forth,
Ever the optimist.
Knowing that life can be better,
I am ready to taste all the sweetness of life.

When Rumi's beloved says,
"I have come all this way, eager for you,"
I knew this day would change the path of my life.
I have come all this way.
I have come
All this way.

My deepest desire is to wake every morning
And have someone whisper,
"Good morning, my love."
That wish was true today,
Being romanced through Rumi.

Although I am uncertain what the rest of the day will be,
For now,
For this morning,
My wish came true.

In the land where fairytales come true,
This is no ordinary day.

Backstory on "No Ordinary Day"
May 11, 2019

The night before I wrote this poem, I had the most epic first date of my life. After moving to Orlando, the happiest place on earth, and waiting a respectable time after the divorce, I was ready to dip my toe into the dating pool. I was fearful, nervous, and wanted to have fun.

My beloved found me. He pursued me. He wined, dined, and danced me to the greatest first date of my life, and I was all in. This date exceeded all expectations.

The next morning, he sent me "Bittersweet" by Rumi.

The entire poem above downloaded in seconds, and each day with him is no ordinary day.

Daydreams

I awoke slowly,
Stretching and lazily becoming alert.
Something resisted,
And I fell back into a
Daydream.

I saw my love standing,
Overlooking a railing,
Sunglasses gleaming,
White shirt radiant
In the Mediterranean sunlight.

I saw him watching
Intently,
As the drudgery of the project
Was proceeding slowly.

Repetitious monotony
Lulling you into a
Daydream.

Suddenly, I saw myself
Standing next to him,
Sunglasses gleaming,

Flowing silk dress
In the Mediterranean breeze.

He moved
To envelope me,
Leaning in
With his hands
On the rail next to mine.

It was as if we
Had done this
A thousand times before
For the first time.

I leaned into him,
His chin next to
My left ear.

My ear gently touching
His face, his beard,
And all the secret
Sensations that only
He knows.

That spot that I
Reserved only for him

Became alive
With his touch.
And just as suddenly,
The daydream
Dissolved,
Dissolved into desire.

Desire to hear his voice.
Desire to feel his touch.
Desire to understand his deepest thoughts.
Desire to know his secrets.
Desire to feel what turns him on.

Pure elemental,
Multidimensional desire.

Impatience.
Impatience with slow pace of his project.
Impatience with distance one-third of the way
Around the world.
Impatience with waiting,
Knowing that
Everything happens in its own right time.

Daydreams
Of him.

Impatient dreams,
Impatient desire.
Dreams of two.
Two who desire.
Two, who, by coming together,
Feel the transformation
Of solitary life
Into shared daydreams.

There is a plan beyond our conscious knowing
That brings two people together
For the next lesson
We need in our lives.
Quantum entanglement
Of daydreams,
Daydreams leading to
Desire.

Daydreams exploring
Possibilities
Of quantum entanglement—
The quantum entanglement
Called love.

Was it real?
Or did I dream?

Backstory on "Daydreams"

I was pursued by an online dating scam artist. Here is his profile: widower, single parent of a teen, works in the oil industry, handsome picture online—most likely of a male model (can you say, catfish?)—born in some foreign country but educated in England, living in the US, and the single most important clue: inconsistent messages in language and style. And you can google their text messages and find them word-for-word, some on "Love Scam Artists" warning websites. The biggest "tell" is after challenging the verbatim texts without attribution, they become angry. Buh-bye.

Stay safe out there. I got a real nice poem out of this experience.

Diving in the Deep End

Why do they call it falling in love?
Who does that?
Not me.

I can understand tumbling into love.
Falling is certainly not me.

When I think of falling,
I think of the type of fall that is sudden
And finds you on your ass
With your feet in the air,
Hurting.

A jolt so hard, you scramble
To pull your senses together.
The stillness that comes after the disorientation
As you pull yourself together.
The "what just happened" kind of fall.

How can that relate to love?
I don't get it
Because I dive into the deep end of love.

A smooth, elegant
Swan dive
Into the deep end of the pool.

When I come up for air,
The sky is bluer,
The clouds are fluffier,
The days slip by easier.

My world shuffles and reorders quickly,
Instantly.
And I find myself on my ass,
With my feet in the air,
Willingly
Submerged in the deep end of love.

Conversation with My Soul

I sat down to meditate
And my soul appeared
To converse with me.

Soul: Good morning, my beloved.
Me: Good morning, my love.

Me: I was reading the bodhicitta and
I read that the alchemy
That comes together
To bring life
Is a gift.

Soul: Life is meant to be passionate and compassionate.
Me: I feel intense passion.
Soul: Good.

Me: I feel compassion in a way I have never felt.
I feel the connection to all living beings.
Soul: Yes.
Me: Is this real?
Soul: Do you want it to be real?
Me: Yes.

Me: Is what I'm feeling real?
Soul: If you feel that it is real,
It is real.

Soul: My dear,
For once in your life,
Trust your feelings.

Me: I trust my intuition.
Soul: Your intuition is in your head.
Step into your body
And stretch the passion you feel
From your heart
Down through all your chakras,
And hook the feeling into your root chakra.
Feel passion.
Soul: Anchor passion in your body.

Me: I feel the energy smooth out now.
Soul: Yes.
Me: I feel intense desire.
Soul: Yes, when two people make love,
When sacred feminine
Conjoins with holy masculine,
A vortex opens to "we,"
The "we" of your souls joined.

We, your souls,
Exchange divine love.

Me: So, my beloved and I have a karmic connection?
Soul: You know the answer to that.
You have had many lives of love together.
This life was for you both to learn lessons
Before coming together.

Soul: We, your souls,
Are happy and proud of you both.
You learned your lessons,
And now divine love has entered in again.

Me: Thank you, thank you, thank you.

And when I opened my eyes,
The swirling lights of guides and angels
Surround me.
I am loved and supported.

I have confirmation that this love,
Between his holy masculine
And my sacred feminine,
Existed before this life.

This love will exist after this life,
And we are reaping the rewards of
The lessons of this lifetime
That we learned so well.

And now we come together
To share love,
Emanating from eternal love.

At the Edge of the Continent

The day arrives
Slowly and gently
At the edge of the continent.

I wake each morning
Facing the sun
As it rises over the Atlantic.

In twilight sleep,
I hear the waves
And they comfort me.

Each new day
Is an adventure
At the leading edge of the continent.

I stand facing the ocean.
All other life on the continent
Is behind me.

I look out,
I wonder,
What will everyone in the world make of today?

This glorious day that the Lord has made.
Ocean blends into sand,
Sand blends into land
In one continuum,
In one integrated whole.

We are given choices,
We make choices.
Individual, momentary choices
That make up a whole lifetime.

Conscious, thoughtful choices.
Unconscious, reflexive choices.
Unconscious conditioning.

Is unconscious conditioning based on expectations?
Are conscious, thoughtful choices
Based on expectations?
In what construct are choices made
On this continent today?

At the edge of the continent,
I expect a good day.
I have a good day.

Seconds to minutes to hours,
Hours to days to years,
The gift of time.
In one continuum,
In one integrated whole,
Seconds become a lifetime.

I look out at the sparkling sea
And see the waves dance,
The gulls play,
And I am comforted.

To know that
In this moment, in this time,
All is well
At the edge of the continent.

Written for George's birthday

Five Men of the Same Name

First it was my father,
The first of his name.
Then, my husband,
Whose father also had the same name.
And then, I gave birth to a male child.
It was our tradition that I named the boys
And so, I named my son Edward, the fifth of his name
In the paternal line.
The joke was that we named our sons after dead kings.
At one point, I was
Ed's daughter,
Ed's wife,
Ed's daughter-in-law,
Ed's mother.
Two deceased, One divorced.
The one who is left shares fifty percent of my DNA,
And stands on the shoulders of all who came before him.
My boss calls me "the Ed-wrangler"
(And assigned me
A particularly "Ed-typical" customer
To wrangle).
And now I'm down three Eds.

Ex

IV
Not III or V.
Originally, this was to be a blank page.
My father-in-law, III, would say,
"What are you writing, a book?
Leave that chapter out."
So, hence this was originally a blank page.
I rethought that.
It's important to remember
A very important step in my healing.
That, for the last two years,
On August 12
At 7:30 p.m., I recited the
Ho'oponopono prayer.
That's the time I got married.
7:30 p.m.
It was supposed to be 7:00 p.m.
Granny Schatz sent me back up the stairs.
Weddings are to happen on the uptick of the clock.
And, so, at 7:30 p.m., I came back down the stairs
To be married.
I found a YouTube video of the Ho'oponopono prayer:
I am sorry.
Please forgive me.

Thank you.
I love you.
And on August 12,
From 7:30 p.m. until 8:30 p.m.,
I bring to mind Ex, aka IV.
I recite this prayer.
I send Ho'oponopono loving-kindness.
The process exhausts me.
I am in bed at 8:32 p.m.
Forgiveness is exhausting.
Augenblick.

One-Sentence Poem

Never date a Tod(d).

It is well known that I am an anti-Toddite. I'm sure their mothers love them. But why name them Tod(d)?

Two-Sentence Poem

Honesty is like virginity.
Once it's gone, there's no turning back.

North Carolina, of Course, North Carolina

In the 499 days,
I got out of North Carolina as much as possible.
I mean I left.
I got out of Dodge.
I raised my hand for work trips.
I went to Orlando
Six times before I moved there.
And, on one of those trips back,
Driving near Savannah,
It hit me.
It was North Carolina.
I went through big life changes
When I was in North Carolina.
I got approval for a mortgage
For the Burkes Drive house.
I quit a job.
I got hired for a job.
I got interviewed for my current job.
There were more things, like a Deloitte interview,
All when I was in North Carolina.
As I drove into South Carolina,
On my way back to the beach house,
It hit me that this
Big change
Had to happen

When I was in North Carolina.
It never would have happened
If I had been living anywhere else.
I don't know what it is
About North Carolina.
But if you want to
Throw your life into
Utter upheaval,
Move to North Carolina.
But batten down the hatches
And close the storm shutters;
You are in for an emotional hurricane.

Boomerang Love

It was a May to December romance.
Not May-December.
We are too old to be May-December.
It started in May
With the most epic date
Of my life.
We were the get-a-room people.
The attraction was hot.
The chemistry was combustible.
And, like fireworks,
We exploded.
Then we fizzled.
Once,
Twice,
Three times
A lady
(Ha-ha, had to add that).
Boomerang Love.
The first time, Roly ghosts me for three days.
I tell him to listen to the song "Boomerang Love."
We both live on different islands.
We vow to try again.
The second time I was sick.
His own stuff made him unavailable to me.

He pulled back.
I trashed all the stuff he gave me.
I'm done.
Three:
My mother died.
I found out when my cousin, Natalie, phoned me.
She, my cousin, the daughter of my aunt who sat with Dad while he passed,
Called me to tell me Emilie had passed.
My sister sent me a Facebook Messenger message.
Facebook. Messenger.
I feel great compassion for my sister.
I'm boo-hooing into the phone with my cousin.
I tell her, "I'm not crying because Mom died.
Mom was ninety. She lived a long (miserable) life.
I'm crying because I miss Rolando."
She says, "Text him."
I text him.
He is so compassionate.
He is so caring.
He tells me what I need to hear,
To get through it all,
Dealing with Sister-Facebook and Sister-Mercurial.
For that, I will forever be grateful.
Thank you, Natalie, too.
Boomerang Love.

He says, "Do you have a nickname for me?"
I say, "Boomerang," and we laugh and laugh.
We go dancing yet again,
And, you guessed it,
Fireworks.
Months of fireworks this time.
Vacations and fireworks.
We were like two magnets,
When they are anywhere
Around each other,
They jump together.
The attraction was that strong.
Until Thanksgiving,
And something he said
Made me quiver deep inside.
Foreshadowing.
I knew it was coming to an end.
Either my intuition was
On high gear
Or men are good at telegraphing intentions.
At least he didn't break it off before Christmas.
He painted several paintings.
Art to fill my walls.
Lovely Christmas Day.
We celebrate New Year's together.
Then crickets started chirping.

Crickets in January.
No morning texts. Crickets.
Days between texts. Crickets.
No calls. Crickets.
Until Yo no puedo más:
I can't take any more.
I, like a bud,
Open to his attention.
When he withdraws
His attention,
I close up.
I don't wither.
Not this time.
I gather nutrients and heal.
Because I deserve better.
This life, our time, was meant to be a
Fleeting passion.
Nothing long term.
Only fireworks.
Burn hot.
Fizzle out.
The timing was all wrong.
I'm running at a high vibration,
Moving along full speed with personal passion projects.
I am unapologetic about the choices I make.
I will no longer make myself small

To fit in.
To fit in with a husband.
To fit in with a romantic interest.
To fit in with work.
He is puttering around in retirement.
High gear cannot coexist with low gear.
I don't want to hear excuses:
"It's too far,
I hate I-4."
If someone wants to be with me,
They will move heaven and earth
To make it so.
I want someone who will
Wrap his romance all around me
Until we kindle a passion
That ignites the love
We deserve
This time around.
With mutual respect,
We end it.
And, paradoxically, my spirit soars.
I am grateful for the way he
Ignited the sacred feminine in me.
I am grateful for the soul connection.
He found me in this life.
He will find me in the next

Only earlier, when we can
Build a life together.
The dissonance of music being played
In two different keys,
At two different speeds,
Was too hard to blend.
It was not our time.
Goodbye, Lisita.
Goodbye, Rolito.
And I put the boomerang in the trash.

My Eulogy to Emilie

Emilie B. Pascovich Nezneski

July 21, 1927–August 16, 2019

Here are some things that I want to remember about my mom:

She was a musician, and probably as good or better than my dad. She played the piano, and the violin.

For some reason known only to her, she would never play in front of anyone.

I remember standing outside the bay window in the front of the house (it's a bay window, not a bow window—Mom would get that), seeing her play something like Bach. And when she saw me, she abruptly stopped, closed the piano, and walked away.

She liked to sing church hymns on the way home from Sacred Heart Church. Loud. At the top of her lungs. I think that's where I get my love of playing music insanely loud in the car.

She liked to drive. I love to drive.

We took some weird adventures. Like the time some Batko cousin died and she and I drove all night to Connecticut to the funeral. And, turns out, it was the second husband of the already-dead Batko cousin. I met some dude named Gus from Forest Hills and we were going to get together at the Forest Hills/Portage football game. Never happened. Sorry, Gus.

I never knew what her middle name that started with a "B" was. We teased her that it was Bertha Butt Boogie. That didn't go over well. But I still laugh.

My mother taught elementary school for fifty-two years. From the age of nineteen to the age of seventy, she was a fixture. Countless students rolled through her classroom.

I mean her Queendom. LOL.

I have memories of three songs that she would sing to me when we did laundry in the basement in a wringer washer:

"Some Sunday Morning"

"How Much Is That Doggie in the Window?"

"How Do You Do, My Partner?"

We didn't have a dishwasher or modern washing machine until circa 1965, the color TV in 1968. I remember watching *I Dream of Jeannie* in color for the first show ever. (And *Batman*.)

When I was in the Junior Miss local pageant, she wrote me a little note to read in between each section of the contest. That was the nicest thing she ever did for me. I remember that fondly.

They did buy me a car after college, and they gave a truck to my son, Edward, and a car (the Rhinoceros) to my son, George. Those vehicles defined their young manhood. I am grateful for all three vehicles.

So, a memory flashed into my head of how totally innocent my mom was. We are standing in Stager's—which was rare because she never did the grocery shopping—and she sees a package of stickers. There were different ones. With delight, she says she's going to hand them out to her students. One is a rhinoceros, complete with a horn. The caption read: *I'm so horny.* I say, "Mom, you can't give those out to kids."

"Why not?" Big argument, and so a Catholic teenager has to explain what horny is to her mother. She did not buy the stickers. Whew.

One time she said to my sons, "I don't know how to talk to a fax machine." They cracked up over that forever.

One time, we as a family, visit. (My ex-husband, unfortunately, never felt welcome.) So, Mom gets confused with all these Eds on the premises: Ed, my dad; Ed, my husband; Ed, my son. She says, "What shall I call you?" to my ex. He says, "Call me Captain," and she totally goes along with it. "Captain, would you like more mashed potatoes?" And we are all cracking up.

So, for all the faults and problems she had in life, I forgave her many years ago. She truly had what she called "Hell on Earth." I know she is in a much better place.

Emilie B. Pascovich Nezneski, thank you for the gift of life. I will do you proud.

Love, Lisa.

Mindful Spilled Coffee

With an unsteady hand,
I spill my coffee
Every morning.

Is it inattention?
Do I overfill the cup
From inattention?

Or perhaps
It is purposeful overfilling,
So that I
Spill my coffee
Every morning.

Backstory on "Mindful Spilled Coffee"

I had to stop drinking coffee in the car because I would show up to work with coffee all over me.

Out of frustration one morning, I lamented, "Why do I do this? Every. Stinking. Morning." And this poem above popped into my head.

Today

Today, my life is better.
Today is filled with so many layers.
Today, I have slowed down my life,
Not because I'm sixty years old.
(I'm not a senior citizen until I choose to be one.)
I have slowed down, though, intentionally to appreciate,
Appreciation for everything and everyone in my life.
Today, I am relaxed.
Today, I am focused.
Today, I better understand concentration and effort.
Today, I better understand myself.
I accept and acknowledge my role in everything,
Everything that happened in my life.
I was there.
My choices, my thoughts, my actions,
I accept it all as a necessary step
To bring me to today.
Today is full of hope and promise
Because each and every moment,
86,400 seconds in today,
Are magical,
Are a gift,
A gift not to be wasted.
I hold in my hand

The power of appreciation of
Today,
And every day forward.

The Year of Becoming

Something clicked.
Something changed.
Permanently for the better.
Sometime after the lentil/termite misadventures,
Things settled down.
No more liminal.
No longer/not yet turned into now.
Living life in the now.
Regular spot for meditation.
Regular visits with my granddaughter.
Ordinary became extraordinary.
Mundane became special.
Frustrations with the loss of my entire universe of work
Because of an "upgrade"
Were managed,
Handled adeptly.
I got a new hairstyle,
A pixie.
I got dressed up to go out.
I enjoyed the Orlando traffic
That takes an hour to go five miles;
I flashed back to Fullerton, California.
I don't mind. There are people here.
There are options and resources

And only one little, black snake.
I named him Harvey.
He eats bugs. He is helpful.
And I began to feel a profound connection
To all living beings.
My personality has become softer
Because I no longer have to fight through the day.
No one blindsides me.
I am in charge of my own future.
I am in charge of my destiny.
I am in charge of now.
Signs become regular.
I feel my energetics open.
I purge every last bit of residual illness I carried with me.
I see life with new eyes.
I see the beauty of nature.
I share the beauty of nature with others.
I ground into Flo-Ri-Dah,
And the sacred manifests in my life.
I start to feel very different.
Vigilance and hypervigilance
That accompanied me for fifty-eight years
Is gone.
Depression has eased so much,
It's hard for me to read my journals.
The time of the depression seems foreign.

I know it was real.
The pain I felt overwhelms me still,
But it is not the pain of current life experiences.
It is no longer real in the now.
I begin to take much better care of me.
I pace myself better.
I swim. I ride a floating unicorn and daydream.
I go on dates.
I buy a new car.
I glance up at the banner I made for myself at Rocky Point.
SITBB. Six Impossible Things Before Breakfast.
It hung at Rocky Point.
It hung in the beach house.
It hung in the RV.
It hangs in my office now
To remind me that I can do the seemingly impossible.
Audrey Hepburn said, "It's I'm possible."
A remarkable lady.
SITBB.
Six Impossible Things
Before Breakfast.
And nearly two years after I took a pause from writing,
Because
My turgid thinking did not lend itself easily
To full sentences,
I begin writing in earnest.

I take two Proprioceptive Writing classes,
One with the renowned author of *Writing the Mind Alive*,
The great thinker, advisor, counsellor, feminist
Linda Trichter Metcalf.
I went on a seven-day silent meditation retreat.
I had a mindful near-death experience
When a red-hot fireball hurtled down my throat
Into my windpipe
As I mindfully looked up
At a snow-covered evergreen tree
In Estes Park, Colorado.
And day by day,
With sunshine as my constant companion,
I see who I've become.
I like her.
I really like her.
I'm really glad that she survived all that chaos.
I'm really glad that, while she lived sad on that island,
She learned to love herself.
I'm really glad that experiences of
Augenblick are regular and routine occurrences.
So many things have much more meaning.
So many other things have less meaning.
The important things are in perspective.
And, I'm really glad that I am still here to tell this story.
I am a survivor.

The fabric of my life is perforated
So I can let all the light in.
The fabric of my life is punctuated
With significant and regular moments.
My greatest hope is that others can benefit from my story.
In addition to loving myself,
I have learned that
I am never alone.

–The End of This Book–

(Not the end of my story, for a long time yet to come.)

About the Author

Lisa Nezneski, B.S. Pharm.D., BCPS, is a leading authority in the field of Integrative Medicine, bringing the benefits of traditional medicine, meditation, and alternative modalities in a well-rounded approach to health and healing. She is a board-certified pharmacotherapist, a mindfulness meditation teacher, professional healthcare consultant, Botanical Medicine specialist, Reiki Master, Intuitive, author, and speaker.

Dr. Nezneski has mastered the skills of communicating wise, fact-based advice that promotes the importance of both medication and meditation in everyday health thanks to her more than thirty years of experience in the dynamic and ever-evolving field of healthcare. As a clinical pharmacist, she served as hospital administrator, strategist, and healthcare consultant to institutions and individuals. She is lovingly known as the Queen of Orphan Drugs at her day job.

She has been a Clinical Professor at Duquesne University, and was the Chief Clinical Officer of Schatz Clinical Services, a consulting company that provided pharmacy services to small hospitals and long-term care facilities. She is currently the owner of Healthy Mindful Self, an integrative medicine company that safely combines medication with natural supplements.

Dr. Nezneski received her Bachelor's degree from the University of Pittsburgh and her Doctor of Pharmacy from the University of Cincinnati. She received her Certification in Botanical Medicine from the University of Western States, an integrative health sciences university. She obtained a certificate in Leadership Essentials from Harvard Business School and a certificate in the McKesson Leadership 201 Program from the Wharton University of Pennsylvania. Her work has been published in numerous professional journals, including the *American Journal of Hospital Pharmacy*. Dr. Nezneski is currently enrolled in the prestigious training program Mindfulness Meditation Teacher Certification through Sounds True.

○ ○ ○

"After denying the pivotal role poetry plays in my life for far too long, I have accepted that I AM a poet. I imbue pieces of myself in my work, in that poetry has allowed me to plunge into the deepest depths, process emotions, and rise above. For me, poetry is alive. Poems course through my veins, enter my lungs, and are exhaled into the world."

○ ○ ○

To download free meditations, go to lisa.nezneski.com.

To receive weekly blogs, go to lisanezneski.com/blog.

Thanks for reading *Grounded in Chaos.* Your opinion matters. I welcome an honest review on Amazon.com. Thank you in advance for your review and for sharing this time with me. Remember, you are never alone.

GROUNDED IN CHAOS

Made in the USA
Columbia, SC
20 May 2021

37640681R00147